EXORCISM

EXORCISM

HOW TO CLEAR AT A DISTANCE A SPIRIT POSSESSED PERSON

by

EUGENE MAUREY

1469 Morstein Road
West Chester, Pennsylvania 19380 USA

ABOUT THE AUTHOR

Rev. Eugene Maurey has been a practicing spiritual healer since 1974. He is a member of the *World Federation of Healing*, London, *The Society for Psychical Research*, London, *The Theosophical Society*, Wheaton, Illinois, and the *The American Society of Dowsers*, Danville, Vermont. He is a stimulating lecturer on unorthodox healing, exorcism, metaphysics, and psychic abilities.

It is not implied that any of the above organizations endorse or accept any or all of the ideas expressed in this book. These are the thoughts and experience of the author and he is totally responsible for what is written here.

Printed in the United States of America.
ISBN: 0-914918-88-5
Published by Whitford Press
A division of Schiffer Publishing Ltd.
1469 Morstein Road, West Chester, Pennsylvania 19380

This book may be purchased from the publisher.
Please include $2.00 postage.
Try your bookstore first.

Dedication

This book is dedicated to Dr. Edward P. Jastram who has selflessly given his time, his energy, and his genius to make this work possible.

Physicians and spiritual healers are often confronted with a client who does not respond to treatment. Such a person may be spirit possessed or under the influence of negative energies. This book describes the effects of these influences on a person and gives a step-by-step method to remove them.

The ideas presented here have originated from many sources. Some have come from the *Catholic Ritual of Exorcism*. Many have come from Peace Pilgrim's knowledge of the spirit world. My conversations and correspondence with leading psychic researcher and author, the late Harold Sherman, has given me a solid base for what is written here. Bill Finch's pioneer work, *The Pendulum and Possession* was an excellent source. I wish to thank the Rev. John Van Drie, of Lansing, Illinois, and Dr. Leonid Kovalevsky of Palos Verdes, California, for their perceptive comments during the preparation of this book. To Rose LeVan, editor of Hypatia Press in Munster, Indiana, I wish to express my gratitude for her able assistance in the intricacies of the English language, as well as for her guidance in the arrangement of this book. To Enid Hoffman, psychic and author, I am most grateful for her encouragement and guidance in the final preparation of this book. Lastly, I am most indebted for direction in this work by the master dowser, scientist and foremost expert in depossession, Dr. Edward P. Jastram of Rehobeth, Mass.

Author's Preface

In 1970 a friend handed me a book with the remark, "This will blow your mind!" The book was the *Secret Science Behind Miracles* by Max Freedom Long. It proved to be a most intriguing book, the first of many I would read on the ancient Hawaiian religion, Huna. This gave me an insight into the spirit world and a hint to the mysteries I would later learn to unravel. About ten years before studying Huna, I met 'the mystic, Peace Pilgrim. She stirred my interest in the spirit world by a chance remark she made when leaving a northside home in Chicago. Frowning, she remarked, "I'm worried about those people".

"Why?" I inquired.

"Well," She replied, "they are members of the *Talking Tongues*.

Curiously, I asked, "What's that?"

She then went on to explain that the members of the sect would gather in a church and seat themselves on the carpeted floor. Music would be played. Shortly afterward some of the members of the congregation would go into a trance, roll on the floor, and begin to speak in foreign languages. Some spoke old English or ancient French, which could be understood. Others spoke languages long forgotten.

I was thoroughly fascinated by Peace's story. I pressed for more details. "How come?" I asked.

She explained, "The phenomenon is caused by recall or possession."

"What's recall?" I persisted.

"They have lived in another lifetime and they are recalling the events of that lifetime," she explained.

"Okay," I responded, "There may be something to reincarnation. But what is possession?" Her answer to that question shook the very foundation of my basic beliefs.

"The spirits of the dead can enter the bodies of the living. When this happens, these members often roll and toss. They are trying to repel the take-over. Later such people can be more easily possessed without being aware of it. It can be very harmful."

For a person who had no religious beliefs or background in religion, the possibility that spirits of the dead could be real threw me into another dimension of thought. I was hooked. I wanted to know more about reincarnation and about spirits who possess people. There were a number of popular books written on reincarnation, one of which was *The Search for Bridey Murphy* by Morey Bernstein. But there was little I could read about possession. It wasn't long before my interest in it waned. Many years later, spirit possession resurfaced in my life with a personal experience. My son became mentally and physically a victim of possession. Not only did his personality become affected, he also suffered a serious illness. Both conditions were eventually healed.

I hope this book will cause you to think. It explains what the Next Dimension or Other Side is all about. It gives the causes and remedy for spirit possession. It provides a practical method to clear the alcoholic of his habit and free the drug user of his need.

This book describes the destructive effects of negative thought energies on others and on ourselves. It provides a simple method of neutralizing these negative energies.

Of greatest importance this book will identify the cause of serious illness making possible a permanent cure rarely achieved by the medical profession.

The subjects covered in this book are controversial. I attribute this to our reluctance to change, to cast aside those ideas which are threatening to our personal security, in conflict with our beliefs or experience. Changes to cultures tend to move very slowly in chronological time. Our cultural devotion and attachment to the "truth" as disclosed by our scientific researchers into the material universe retards our investigation of the invisible world.

Fifty-five years ago hypnotism was scorned when I was first introduced to it. My interest in hypnotism started in 1933 when William Osner, a retired shoe manufacturer and scholar related to me his incredible experience as a hypnotist. He described his hypnotized subject believing and acting out unusual situations. There were those who forgot their names; others could not bend their arms or legs. Some were made to believe that the floor was burning hot, compelling them to climb upon a chair. Others in deep trance could not feel a needle through their hand or would point to objects hidden in the room.

To me this was fun and games. As a curious teenager, I was fascinated. After studying a small book on the subject, I was soon able to hypnotize my brother, my sister and many of my close friends.

A half century ago, most psychologists and psychiatrists would have nothing to do with hypnotism. Most were certain that it did not exist; others maintained that it had no value. At that time, hypnotism was classified as a trick used by stage magicians in their acts. It was a taboo subject.

As my interest in hypnotism increased, I searched for books on the subject in the main downtown Chicago Public Library. In those early years, not a single book could be found! Today, they can be counted in the hundreds.

In the large city libraries it is difficult to find a book describing how spirit possession is cleared or exorcised. There are few individuals who acknowledge that spirit possession occurs, and even fewer who know what to do about it.

Libraries today have little literature on the subject of possession. There is nothing that covers exorcism performed at a distance from the client. This book will fulfill the urgent need for information on the subject, near or at a distance.

It is my earnest desire that it will not be long before there is a general acceptance that spirit possession exists and that it can be treated. After the invading spirits are exorcised, the value to the victim is substantial. When the worth of an exorcism becomes more widely recognized as with hypnotism, I am certain that this process will be accepted and will do much to alleviate the suffering of many of our fellow humans.

The ideas presented in this book may first appear to be fantastic to you. When you comprehend what is written here and put to test the instructions given, you too, will be able to demonstrate extraordinary results.

Contents

What Is An Exorcism?

A Miracle?... The Vigilant Farmer's Dog... The Safe Divorce. What Happens When A Person Dies?... Life After Life... The Other Side of Death... Recollections of Death, Arthur Ford's Survival... The Normal Death Experience... Wrong Way Spirit. Peace Pilgrim, Mystic.

PART ONE
THE THEORY OF POSSESSION AND EXORCISM

The Teacher... The Catholic Church on Possession... The Case of Father Surin... Cardinal Appoints Six Exorcists.. .The Pope Participates... The Traditional Exorcism... Looking Back... Other Practices.

Bill Cox's Method... Reading the Pendulum... Parametric Analysis Chart... American Society of Dowsers... The Analysis... Our Limitations... Healing Blocks... A Measure of Evaluation... Probing the Subconscious... Negative Programming... Frustration... Health... Wholeness.

Wiping the Slate Clean... Not Her Problem!... The Scientist... The Compassionate Exorcist... Evaluation of Spirit Entities... The Freeway Killer.

My Method of Clearing... Getting the Answers... Be Gentle... Not with Kid Gloves... Van Drie's Clearing Method... Mass Clearing... Self-Clearing... The Lesson.

The Gang... The Cult Builder... Who is the Murderer? Coleman-Brown, Killers... The Three Faces of Nancy... The Night Stalker... Parole Officer, Skeptic... The Highjackers... Terrorism... A Moral Problem?... The Killer Within... The Suicidal Personality... A Challenge.

Visualization and Thought Forms... Seeing Is Believing... Negative Energies... Ancient Spells... Power of Spells... Hexing in Our Time... The Doll and the Witch... How to Neutralize a Hex... How to Change a Person... Expectancy... Detecting Negative Energies... Clearing Negative Energies... Protection... Further Thoughts.

Your Power... Power of Love... Rescue Work... Harmony... Spiritual Healing... A Look Into the Future... Frontiers.

Introduction

What Is An Exorcism?

Can a negative and troublesome person change and become cheerful and loving? From fifteen years of research and study, my conclusion is an emphatic "Yes!" Furthermore, I have found that a profound personality change can take place virtually overnight. In fact, the simple method described in this book will produce amazing results. The alcoholic suddenly turns away from the bottle. The violent husband becomes a loving one. The drug user thrusts aside his narcotics and pills. The intended suicide forgets his self-destructive impulses. The hypochondriac no longer has a day of illness.

Many people exhibit more than one personality, each one distinctly different from the other. They appear to be two or more people in a single physical body. My experience in thousands of case studies indicate that more than eighty percent of such multiple personalities are a result of spirit possession. Spirit, in this context refers to a dead person who still has all the mental, emotional and personality characteristics he had when alive. Possession occurs when a disembodied spirit takes control of the mind and body of a living person.

A MIRACLE?

This book is about the exorcism or clearing of people who are spirit possessed. It is not about demons or the devil if such exists. This is a "How to Do It" book. It will teach you to perform an exorcism safely in a few minutes. Furthermore, you need not be in the presence of your client when you do the work. There is nothing of a sensational nature written here except the results. *The results are sensational.* In fact, what you will be able to do will often be called a miracle. It is not a miracle. It is only a miracle for those who don't understand what happened - what you caused to happen.

This book will take you in pathways that you may not yet have traveled. In your process of discovery, you will learn what spirit possession is, you will learn to recognize it instantly, and you will know how to overcome it. You will become acquainted with the world identified as the Other Side. You will understand the laws which govern it. You will also know how to deal with it, safely and effectively. You will come to know your way around that world.

To illustrate what can be accomplished by using the instructions detailed in this book, the following two cases are given.

THE VIGILANT FARMER'S DOG

About a year ago a farmer, Mr. Barry 0. wrote to me from New Zealand. The date was omitted.

"I have been reading the August edition of the *Faithist Journal* and your article rang a bell. For some time now, by my very actions and thoughts towards my fellow human beings close and not so close to me, I have felt I've been directed by some outside force. I haven't found any answers with religion and there must be more in life than what I've found so far.

"Please remove the unwanted spirits from our family."

Mr. 0. supplied a list giving the name and age of each member of his family, including his own. For good measure he added his horse and 4 dogs! Upon examination (using the method explained in this book) it was found that Mr. 0. was being controlled by 3 intelligent alien entities and had attracted an additional 32 who were nearby. This is a typical profile of an alcoholic, although it is possible that Mr. 0. was not an alcoholic. Also, his sixteen year old daughter, Mavis, was being influenced by a weak negative entity. The rest of the family, including the horse and dogs, were clear of spirit entities. On November 6, 1987, Mr. 0. and Mavis were cleared using the distant technique explained in this book.

On Mar. 2, 1988, I received the following letter from Mr. 0.

"Thank you very much for your help. For the first time I can think with a single mind rather than as a man with two minds, with very little control over either. I had become so negative I was becoming physically blind.

"It is summer time for hay making. I cut the hay paddocks in a different pattern, also baled the hay in without a breakdown. It was the best hay season I've ever had; did the job in half the time. Before 8th Nov.'87, my mind was as though it was on a roller coaster and I didn't know how to stop or get off.

"My daughter, Mavis, was home for Christmas. She's a different person, brighter, more go and feels great."

Mr. O. then described an incident which probably occured at the time of the exorcism.

"After writing to you the first time and waiting to receive your report, things started to happen to me. One morning at 5 AM, I was awaken to the sound of Tab, our dog, running around the side of the house barking at something. As I lay in bed, I felt as though a giant vacuum was sucking the air out to the west corner of the house; pulling the spirits from within the house? I don't know, but our dog was aware there was something happening at that moment."

Mr. 0. then went on to relate an incident which occurred shortly afterwards on November 9, 1987. The 9th was a few days after the date of the clearing which had been done at a distance of approximately 12,000 miles. The country where Mr. 0. resides is rugged and mountainous and the roads often turn abruptly. Driving around a bend on such a road after a violent storm, he suddenly came upon a large fallen tree across the road and collided with it. His car was severely damaged but he escaped without hurt. Such accidents with resulting injury had all too often been his lot. He attributed his miraculous escape to what had occurred to him a few days earlier when his mind had suddenly cleared wiping off all negative thinking.

THE SAFE DIVORCE

The second case, not so distant as New Zealand, is noteworthy in illustrating the startling results of an exorcism. The first letter written by Margaret M. from California is dated August 24, 1987. The first paragraph of the letter, indicating where the writer had heard of me, is omitted.

"It is very important for our family, before other (perhaps too radical) steps are taken, to know whether the person whose name I give below is harboring an attached entity."

The name of Burr A., age 66, was given.

A P.S. was added. "This is our beloved, eldest son-in-law. He has become unstable in behavior (rages). We want to help our daughter if we can. She is helpless to know how to help him and would be very grateful for any input you can give."

My analysis indicated that the son-in-law indeed had a serious problem. A strong malevolent entity was almost in total control of him. A person with such an intruder on board would typically be physically violent and also, more than likely, be suicidal. On September 3, 1987 he was cleared, and the entity, with an entourage of about thirty, was sent on his way. Several months later, on January 4, 1988, I received the following letter from Margaret M.

"Thank you for the excellent work you did for our son-in-law, Burr A.

"I received your report just before Christmas. But the good effects of it were quite apparent months before, especially at the time when he was served with the divorce papers, November 21st. (from previous observation, this would have caused him to become violent and murderous). The miracle, the opposite happened. He did go into a kind of shock, but became cooperative and to a certain extent, even helped my daughter to move. But the best was that all of us involved had by then somehow lost our fear of his 'blowing up' when he was faced with those legal papers.

"It is all so gratifying that he is coping. How can we thank you enough!"

In Chapter 11 we will examine and identify forces, other than intelligent alien entities, which can seriously harm a person. You will be able to neutralize such forces and bring about startling changes for the better.

WHAT HAPPENS WHEN A PERSON DIES?

To understand what actually happens when a person becomes possessed, it is necessary to have an understanding of the nature of death and a clear picture of the spirit world. Once we begin to understand what it is like on the Other Side and know something about the laws which govern that state of being, we can arrive at conclusions and simple solutions involving intruding spirits.

The medical profession has made extensive inquiry into the process of death which provides us with a good insight as to what happens when we die. Although the experiences related by medical doctors and scientists may conflict with some religious beliefs, it is not the purpose of this book to enter into a religious discussion or controversy.

LIFE AFTER LIFE

The eminent physician, Dr. Raymond A. Moody in his book, *Life After Life* records many near-death (NDE) experiences. He sums up the experience of dying as follows:

As a man is dying he finally reaches the point of release. He hears his doctor pronounce him dead. He then finds himself outside of his physical body, yet with all the mental alertness of when alive. He may linger for a short while in the immediate vicinity of the physical body but then find himself traveling swiftly through what appears to be a long dark tunnel. Usually it is a pleasant journey toward a warm loving light.

In the place he now finds himself, others come to meet and help him. He may glimpse friends and relatives who have already died.

A warm and loving being identified with the light asks him to evaluate his life and shows him an instantaneous presentation of the major event of his life. This gives him serious reflection on the accomplishments and failures of his earthly life.

For the person who must return to the world of the living, he now finds that he likes this new environment and is reluctant to return. He finds himself free of pain, light of body and in an environment of love and peace. He often will resist returning to the physical body but soon finds that he has no choice but to return and live.

Dr. Moody concludes, "The experience affects his life profoundly, especially his views about death and its relationship to life."

Dr. Moody finds a recurring theme of disbelief and skepticism by those hearing a person's near-death experience (NDE).

When the patient recovers, he tries of tell others of his most wonderful unearthly experience. He often encounters skepticism and even ridicule and soon stops telling his story. The near death experience invariably has a profound influence on his belief of life after death. The positive aspect of such an experience often gives new direction to his purpose in life.

THE OTHER SIDE OF DEATH

C.W. Leadbeater, distinguished Theosophist, in his book, *The Other Side of Death*, adds this to the experience of dying:(p. 25)

"This process of transition from one world to another is in no sense painful; we should dismiss from our minds all thought of suffering in connection with death. There may indeed be suffering before death, on account of disease or accident, but the actual process of death is not only painless, but usually full of joy and peace." Leadbeater continues:

"The physical element relinquishes its hold reluctantly upon the body, so that body sometimes struggles for breath. The dying person is unconscious of that struggle and feels only the wonderful lightness, relief, and freedom from the heavy burden of the flesh.

"Shortly after death, the major events of his lifetime on earth flash with lightning rapidity through the consciousness of the ego. In that instantaneous review he sees his life as a whole. He realizes what was intended for him to do in life. He knows how far he has or has not taken his opportunities to fulfill his destiny. He distinguishes clearly for the first time the successes and failures, the victories and defeats, the wisdom or poor judgment of all that he has done and said."

RECOLLECTIONS OF DEATH

Another medical doctor who has researched in depth the experience of dying is Dr. Michael B. Sabom, MD, cardiologist at Atlanta's Veteran's Administration Medical Center and assistant professor of medicine at Emory University. He comments in the January 16, 1983 edition of *Family Weekly* about his initial skepticism, and ultimate acceptance of near-death experiences, (NDE).

"Up until seven years ago, I had never heard of near death experiences even though, as a resident in cardiology, I was caring daily for resuscitated cardiac patients. I then read Dr. Raymond Moody's noted book, *Life After Life* which describes the NDE's of 150 people. My initial impression: 'Utterly ridiculous!' To confirm my skepticism, I, along with psychiatric social worker, Sarah Kreutziger, began talking with patients of our own who had been 'brought back.' Much to my surprise, some told me of near-death experiences which they had not shared before for fear of ridicule. Intrigued, Sarah and I began to study systematically the NDE and over the next five years we talked to 116 patients who had suffered near-fatal medical crises."

Dr. Sabom was astonished to discover that 43 percent of the patients resuscitated from a near death crisis were able to describe a near death experience (NDE). He found that the people reporting the NDE did not differ in religion, sex, age or occupation from the group who had no recollection during their period of unconsciousness.

Dr. Sabom's book, *Recollections of Death,* records the details his patients reported who had a NDE. Typically they described a brilliant source of light which signaled the end of the dark region or void and the beginning of a transcendental environment of great beauty. 'Movement' was toward this light and away from the region of darkness. Under questioning by Dr. Sabom, a 56-year-old executive, Mr. E. from Florida described the light this way: (p. 43)

Mr. E. "I went through this period of darkness. There was this light, like someone holding a flashlight, and I started going towards that. And then the whole thing brightened up and the next thing I remember I was floating. We were going through this shaft of light, the light kept getting brighter and brighter. It was so bright, and the closer we got, the brighter it got. It was blinding."

Dr. S. "Was it irritating?"

Mr. E. "No. There was no part of the experience that was irritating."

Mr. E. further described the light as bright but not producing a shadow. He felt that he was not really looking at the light but was in the light.

There were numerous descriptions of persons being met by friendly beings or relatives during the NDE. A 43-year-old man talked about his postoperative cardiac arrest.

He described coming to a place where he met all his relatives who had died, his grandmother, grandfather, father and an uncle who had recently committed suicide. They were dressed in long gowns with hoods over their heads and were very pleased to see him. Suddenly they turned their backs to him and his grandmother turned her head toward him and said, "We'll see you later, but not this time!"

ARTHUR FORD'S SURVIVAL

Arthur Ford, famous medium and founder of SPIRITUAL FRONTIERS FELLOWSHIP, relates his experiences on the Other Side when he became clinically dead and later revived. (*The Life Beyond Death* by Arthur Ford, pp. 143-146)

"One of the most vivid experiences of my entire life was, in fact, a journey into the higher realms. Some years ago I had an experience that forever lifted this whole matter of survival out of the realm of faith and brought it clearly down to the plane of realism, so far as I am concerned."

Ford related his experience when he was hospitalized for a serious illness and there clinically died. He found himself floating in the air above his bed. He could see his body but had no interest in it. He had a feeling of peace, a sense that all was well. He then blanked out and when he recovered consciousness he found himself floating through space without effort. He knew that he did not possess a body as he had known it, yet there was no question that it existed.

Ford then related his observation of the brilliant illumination of his surroundings as well as the colors he found impossible to describe. He met many of his old friends and astonishingly remarked, "Some, who had passed on in old age were now young, and some who had passed on while children had now matured!"

He found that everyone was busy. They seemed very happy and were occupied with what he termed, "mysterious errands and tasks." Of particular interest were those with whom he had close ties in the past. Now they were no longer interested in him. Others whom he had known only slightly became his constant companions. This seemed natural to him as he knew that the laws of affinity determined his relationships on that side.

When he was directed to return to his body he strenuously objected. He wanted nothing to do with that "beaten, diseased hulk he had left behind in a Coral Gables hospital". Suddenly he found himself hurling through space. He opened his eyes and found himself looking into the face of a nurse. He had been in a coma for more that two weeks.

Arthur Ford recovered from this illness to go on with his life in a new direction. It was at this time that he founded SPIRITUAL FRONTIERS FELLOWSHIP. He made his transition in 1971.

THE NORMAL DEATH EXPERIENCE

The experience of dying as described by Drs. Moody and Sabom as well as by Arthur Ford is similar to hundreds of stories told in dozens of books on the subject. It is almost a format. The consciousness lifts and floats above the lifeless body. Shortly after death there is a review of the highlights of one's life. There is movement through a tunnel with the inevitable warm, loving light at the far end beckoning to the person. The light gives the feeling of being in the presence of a loving friend. The person meets his loved ones who wait with outstretched hands. This is the normal process of dying and it should be emphasized that most people will stay in their new environment and will not return to this earth plane. In 1963 The Mormon Church in Salt Lake City, Utah, showed a special movie in which depicts almost the identical scene.

WRONG WAY SPIRIT

Let us now examine what happens when the normal process of dying does not occur, when the spirit person becomes earthbound, a disembodied spirit. This is the exception rather than the rule. The spirit person is not attracted to the light and becomes cut off from loving friends or from a guide who could help him. In the worst case he finds himself in complete darkness. Such a spirit is said to be in the lower astral plane. This plane is near the surface of the earth. It is populated by earthbound spirits both human and non-human.

What happens to a person when he dies is largely determined by what he thinks when living. On the other side as here, the individual has free will. His new experiences will be governed by his beliefs. A spirit person in the lower astral plane may have during his or her lifetime strongly rejected any concept of an existence after dying. Also, as a disembodied spirit, such person may still have an earthly attachment to some living person, a possession, or a sensual gratification. This can be a powerful incentive to interrupt the normal process of dying.

At first the 'dead' person, not knowing what to expect, is somewhat confused. Such a spirit person has all the same mental faculties when living, yet no longer can communicate with friends or loved ones on earth. Living friends do not answer when he talks to them. In fact, he soon discovers that he cannot be seen. For a person who had no belief about what may happen after death, this experience can be shattering.

Soon such a spirit person finds he must shift for himself. He may take any of several courses of action. he may decide to stay in the home where he was most comfortable when on earth, he may take up residence at his favorite bar or he may visit a friend. Unfortunately, he may remain in the hospital where he died or in the cemetery where his body was interred. He has become an earthbound spirit entity, often referred to as a disembodied spirit, a person without a physical body. As an English General once said on such an occasion, "But if I am dead, where am I? If this is heaven, I don't think much of it; and if this is hell, it is better than I expected!"

PEACE PILGRIM, MYSTIC

Peace Pilgrim had dedicated her life to promote peace among nations and among individuals and to further an understanding of inner peace. She traveled throughout the 50 states lecturing at schools, churches, civic groups and frequently was on television and radio. She had a profound understanding of the mysteries of life. She understood and lived as one with all things, as unity with God. Not only were her acts that of a mystic, it could be said that she was the definition of a mystic.

Peace Pilgrim, was the first to explain to me the process of dying. When she was at the bedside of a person who was dying, she would clairvoyantly see the soul of the person rise above the bed. Often they were confused and frightened by their new state of being. Peace would then calmly explain to the newly released spirit what was happening and what to expect. She would explain the coming review of the major events of the person's life. She would describe the darkened tunnel, the loving warm light and the welcome of the loved ones at the end of the tunnel. Fear and anxiety in the dying process were thus diminished.

I recommend the book written about her, *Peace Pilgrim.* See the bibliography at the end of this book.

This subject is certainly not new but has a long history of discovery. From earliest time there has been reports of spirits interfering with the lives of the living and an exorcism of sorts being performed. To better appreciate the scope and importance of this subject, we will examine in the next chapter significant events that forms the basis of our knowledge of possession and how is was dealt with in the past.

The Theory of Possession and Exorcism

CHAPTER 1
Traditional
View of Possession

The knowledge of possession has been around for centuries.

Books dealing with mythology and histories of the Dark Ages are full of accounts of demonic possession and the ruthless means used to stamp it out. Very little understanding was given to it. The methods to eradicate it were ineffectual. In the traditional meaning, possession is defined today as it was thousands of years ago - an invasion by a demon of a person's body and soul.

THE TEACHER

Jesus of Nazareth was perhaps the most publicized exorcist the world has ever known. There are numerous stories in the Bible of Jesus commanding a demon to leave a person. In Mark 1 the following story is told:

In the town of Capernaum at the synagogue where Jesus was preaching 'a man possessed by a demon was present and began shouting, 'Why are you bothering us, Jesus of Nazareth? Have you come to destroy us demons? I know who you are, the Son of God!'

'Jesus curtly commanded the demon to say no more and to come out of the man. At that the evil spirit screamed and convulsed the man violently and then left him.' When the story was told to the people in the town, it wasn't long before a crowd gathered, many to ask for Jesus' help.

'That evening, Jesus healed a great number of the sick and ordered many demons to come out of their victims. He refused to allow the demons to speak, because they knew who he was.'

In Mark 9, Jesus was shown a boy whose father declared, 'Teacher, I brought my son for you to heal. he can't talk because he is possessed by a demon. And whenever the demon is in control of him, it dashes him to the ground and makes him foam at the mouth and grind his teeth and become rigid. So I begged your disciples to cast out the demon, but they couldn't do it.'

'Jesus turned to his disciples and said, 'Oh what little faith you have. How much longer must I be with you until you believe? How much longer must I be patient with you?' Turning back to the father, he directed, 'Bring the boy to me.'

'So they brought the boy, but when he saw Jesus the demon convulsed the child horribly, and he fell to the ground writhing and foaming at the mouth.

'How long has be been this way?' Jesus asked the father.

'The father replied, 'Since he was very small. The demon often makes him fall into fire or into water to kill him. Oh, have mercy on us and do something if you can.'

'If I can?' Jesus asked. 'Anything is possible if you have faith.'

'When Jesus saw the crowd was growing he rebuked the demon.

'O demon of deafness and dumbness,' he said, 'I command you to come out of this child and enter him no more!'

'Then the demon screamed terribly and convulsed the boy again and left him. The boy lay there limp and motionless, to all appearance dead.' Jesus then took the boy by the hand and helped him to his feet.

The simple methods then employed by Jesus to clear a person has given way to complicated, ritualistic performances that only few now know how to do.

THE CATHOLIC CHURCH ON POSSESSION

Perhaps there is no better documentation dealing with exorcism than that of the Roman Catholic Church. From the time of Jesus of Nazareth, there is constant reference to possession and to those actively engaged in exorcism. During the Inquisition a charge of possession was a one-way road to an execution.

In the Tenth Cannon of the Council of Antioch, held in 341 AD, the then existing Christian church ordained priests to perform exorcisms. The Roman Catholic Church of today has a detailed ritual of exorcism. Before an exorcism is attempted, the Church demands rigid tests and personal interviews to determine if the candidate is indeed possessed. Today, they would rather not deal with it, nor publicize it. Let us go back in time when possession, always considered as by a demon, was a primary responsibility of the Church.

THE CASE OF FATHER SURIN

The official view has been expounded by Jean Lhermitte, in his book *True and False Possession*. Originally, the work was published in France under the title *Vrais et Faux Possedes*. The book has become Volume 43 of the *Twentieth Century Encyclopedia* of Catholicism.

The traditional viewpoint is characterized by Lhermitte using the autobiography of the exorcist, Father Surin, a Jesuit priest who lived in the 17th Century. (pp. 95-97) The mental anguish described by Fr. Surin differs little from today's possessed person.

Fr. Surin arrived in Lundon in 1675 during a critical time when all the churches were occupied by exorcists and where huge crowds were watching what was happening. Unfortunately the good priest was ill suited or prepared for the role of exorcist.

After he had cleared the possessed Sister Jeanne of the Angels, he found that he had taken over the devilish personality that he had removed from her. The diabolical influence invading his mind provoked such violence that he exclaimed, 'The temptations almost drove me mad!' He felt as if he were two persons.

For a man who closely followed the doctrine of his church, he knew that he was possessed by something entirely alien to his real being. So completely was Fr. Surin controlled by this other personality that he explained, 'If I wish to make the sign of the cross on my lips, the other forcibly snatches my hand away and seizes my finger with my teeth to bite me with fury.' Fr. Surin was finally judged by his fellow Jesuits to be mentally unbalanced and placed in an institute for the insane.

M. Lhermitte tells of a similar phenomena of possession. One of his female clients when depressed heard a male voice in the middle of the night speaking. He directed her to kill her child, then but a few months old. The woman was horrified and most distressed but merely told her husband what the 'demon' had said. A few nights later the demon whispered in her ear, 'Kill it!, kill it!' After a few moments of resistance, she seized the child from its cradle and threw it out of the second floor window! Fortunately the child was but slightly injured. The mother was given electric shock treatments and eventually recovered her sanity.

From my experience, the manifestations of possession as related by Fr.Surin are as true today as they were in the 17th Century. There is one fundamental difference held in the modern viewpoint. The devil does not possess; unclean spirits of the dead do. It is possible, however, that some of the evil spirits encountered in my work, could well 'represent' the devil. As we progress in this work, the reasons for this viewpoint will become clear.

CARDINAL APPOINTS SIX EXORCISTS

Today the Catholic Church is still responding to the victims of possession. A news item in the Chicago Tribune, dated February 23, 1986 verifies the Church's continued war against the devil.

'The devil has been far too busy in Turin, so the city's archbishop, Anastasio Cardinal Ballestrero, has appointed six exorcists to battle the Prince of Darkness.

'The appointments were long overdue. No one has officially practiced the art of casting out devils since Turin's last two exorcists retired almost three years ago, both fatigued and in failing health.

'Perhaps coincidental, when the priests retired was precisely the time when Satan became active again in a city reputed for generations to be a bastion of witchcraft and black magic.

'A law student, Gianluigi Corelli, who was doing research in the Turin archdiocese, discovered that over the last three years 1,350 local residents had knocked on parish doors claiming to be possessed by the devil.

'The main task of the six exorcists will be to study a phenomenon that has become increasingly relevant,' Cardinal

Ballestrero said in announcing his appointments. He continued, 'Naturally we do not accept the idea that all those who turn to the church for help against demons are, in fact, possessed. But we have decided to look into this.'

'In nominating his exorcist unit, the cardinal said two of its members were priests and the others were friars. Their ages range from 48 to 70 and, he added, 'Each is endowed with a fine education and an iron constitution.'

'Of those cases reported last year, 16 suffered from symptoms that may have been the result of being possessed by demons. Church sources say of those 16, eight were successfully exorcised. The others apparently remain in the clutches of the devil. But for the Church, that is eight souls too many. With six eager new exorcists, Satan is facing tough times in Turin.'

I feel strongly that the Roman Catholic Church is closing its eyes to the number of person who are possessed. In my experience, by simply counting heads in any group of people, the probability is that I will find at least 1 person in 12 who is possessed. In a group involved in the occult, the ratio jumps to 1 in 6. In some groups, such as in a prison population, the ratio is higher than 1 in 2. These are conservative figures.

THE POPE PARTICIPATES

Derk Kinnane Roelofsma reporting from the Vatican, in Rome posted the following significant story:
'The attractive young woman stood with her mother and her mother-in-law in the high ceiling room in the Vatican. They were nervous that day in Lent 1985. As Pope John Paul II entered the room, the young woman hid behind a sofa. The door closed on the group, but the resonant voice of the Vicar of Christ could be heard through the door, praying in Latin.'

It can be assumed that the Pope followed the traditional exorcism liturgy in which the exorcist prays to aid a person troubled by an invading spirit. The solemn rite of exorcism reads in part: 'I cast thee out, thou unclean spirit, along with the least encroachment of the wicked enemy, and every phantom, and diabolical legion. In the name of our Lord Jesus Christ, depart and vanish from this creature of God.'

It was reported by a senior Vatican official that the Pope told him that it was a new biblical experience for him, one which involved the proximity of an evil spirit.

THE TRADITIONAL EXORCISM

Today, the exorcism practiced in many churches differs little from that of Father Surin's time. The traditional method is described by Dr. M. Scott Peck, M.D. in his book, *People of the Lie.*

Dr. Peck advised on the necessity of using a prepared team with adequate scheduled time before tackling an exorcism. One of his patients had to be restrained for two hours during an exorcism. Another had required almost continuous restraint for more than a day!

If the physical struggle would not dissuade you from participating in an exorcism, the following description of a traditional ritual should. Dr. Peck described a physical encounter with a diabolical entity. (P.196)

'When the demon finally spoke clearly in one case, an expression appeared on the patient's face that could be described only as satanic. It was an incredibly contemptuous grin of utter hostile malevolence. I have spent many hours before a mirror trying to imitate it without the slightest success.'

It was also my unhappy experience to have encountered such an odious character (See The Freeway Killer, Chapter 8). The expression of intense hatred and threat of harmful action I also found difficult to describe adequately.

Dr. Peck's experience coincides with that of Spiritualists, who have regular sessions in which exorcisms are performed. These churches all deal directly with the invading spirit, pitting the exorcist as the opponent of the spirit entity. Communication with the spirit is made through a medium or through the mediumship ability of the subject or host body. This direct approach often leads to the subject becoming violent, frequently causing injury to the exorcist and his helpers. Not always will the exorcist succeed, in fact, there is real danger to him as the evil spirit may jump into him! Rev. Loraine Schulz tells of her role as a helper during such a church exorcism.

'Sometimes we would get a subject who would become so violent that it would take four of us to restrain him. This struggle would go on for hours until the person would become docile and would no longer fight us. After the end of such a session, I would be exhausted and black and blue from the beating I took.'

LOOKING BACK

In each period of man's recorded history there has been a concept of a spirit world. The ancient Egyptians believed in the nether regions where life continues in the after-world. The region was held to exist beneath the earth's surface. There, a spirit person needed much the same support as required on the earth plane. In addition, god-like deities were created to symbolize spiritual values. These gods, represented by a figure, half human, half animal, were said to exist in that other world. There were both good and bad gods.

Those priests who could dispel the evil ones were respected and held in high esteem by the citizenry. Throughout the legends and myths of time, other civilizations far removed and seemingly having no connection with Egypt, followed similar rituals.

OTHER PRACTICES

Polynesia comprises the islands scattered over the southeastern Pacific ocean within the vast triangle formed by the state of Hawaii to the north, New Zealand to the south and Easter Island to the east. In this extensive area the Polynesians practiced a religion known to the Western World as Huna.

The belief in spirits played a strong part in the practice of the Huna religion. The spirits of the dead were used by the Kahuna priests to perform special functions for them. For example, when a new temple was to be built, a slave was buried alive at each corner of the foundation. It was believed that their spirits would forever protect the structure. It was not infrequent that a Kahuna employed the spirits he controlled to kill a person who had caused him displeasure. (Refer to the *Secret Science Behind Miracles* by Max Freedom Long.)

Witchcraft, Voodooism, Satanism, and other religions use the mystery of the spirit world to attract and control their worshipers. Each has its witch doctor, its wizard, its shaman, to remove undesirable spirits from its members. Unfortunately, some have the knowledge of how to attach a spirit entity on a person they wish to punish. Others are skilled in the practice of hexing. As the influences of these religions and practices vitally effect our society today, I cover the subject more fully in Chapter 11.

In this country the Puritans in the 17th Century had their methods to exorcise those suspected of demonic possession.

One method was to use a teeter-board arrangement with a chair at one end. The suspect was tied to the chair and men on the other end dunked the victim in the river! If he/she lived - a rare event - the suspect was declared cleared of demonic influence.

One effective method practiced at the turn of the century to exorcise a suspect was to apply a static spark of electricity at the base of the spine. The spark was then advanced up the spine to the neck. Certainly the patient must have suffered considerable agony.

Apparently, spirits do not like the sensation of electricity and leave the victim when is applied. This has similarity to the electric shock treatment successfully used in treating schizophrenia.

Experiments are going on today with low voltages, hardly felt, being applied to the subject. This is showing promise of becoming a useful tool in clearing a person of personality interference. On the other hand, such a treatment may do more harm than good. The spine is vital to our health. Interfering with the neural connections can affect the brain. There is a possibility of spine damage or spine dislocation. The spine is the main channel of nerves which control the functions of the body. These nerves essentially are the conduit for tiny electrical currents.

Jesus admonished his disciples to teach, heal and to cast out unclean spirits' from the possessed. The meaning of unclean spirits has come down to us to mean demonic spirits. This is not the meaning I give to the negative possessing spirits being exorcised. I identify such spirits as persons who once lived on this earth. They may have demonic characteristics. They have not yet reached a level of spirituality acceptable to society. They are at a low level of morality.

It is conceivable that there may be entities of a lower evolutionary order, invisible to the human eye, that could be classified as demons. In my examination of about 8000 persons I have not encountered an entity identifiable as a demon.

Let us now examine the paradox that the group most to benefit by an understanding of the principles of spirit possession is the first to reject its validity. This is the medical profession. The next chapter explains how the condition described by psychiatrists as a Multiple Personality Disorder obliterates any thought of spirit possession.

CHAPTER 2

The Medical
Viewpoint

There are differing widely held views as to just what spirit possession is. Is it the same as a Multiple Personality Disorder (MPD)? The medical profession defines a person with MPD as one who exhibits more than one personality and that they coexist and can alternate in control of the physical person.

PSYCHIATRISTS' VIEWS ON MULTIPLE PERSONALITIES

Psychiatrists are not in complete agreement with one another about what causes a multiple personality disorder (MPD). Dr.Frank Putnam, a psychiatrist at the National Institute of Mental Health and a leading researcher in the field of multiple personalities has this to say: (Report from the International Society for the Study of Multiple Personality & Dissociation Conference of 1985.)

'The multiple personality offers a special window into psychosomatics. With a multiple personality you can do research that holds the body constant while you vary the personality, so that you can sort out how psychological states affect the body.

'Multiples exhibit some remarkable medical phenomena. A patient may react normally to a sedative drug in one personality, but is not affected by it in another personality. It is as if they were two different people.'

In the above conference Dr. Bennett Braun, who directs a unit devoted to treating multiple personalities at Rush-Presbyterian-St. Luke's Medical Center in Chicago reports:

'Some multiples carry several different eyeglasses, because their vision changes with each personality. One case was of a young woman who in one personality was color blind for blue and green, a problem that ended with the successful treatment of her multiple personality condition.

'Another woman, admitted to a hospital for diabetes, baffled her physicians by showing no symptoms of the disorder when one personality, who was not diabetic, was dominant. A young man was allergic to citrus fruit in some personalities, but not in others.

'Research on brain patterns of multiples has produced data of unusual promise. In the case of a woman, who at one point in her treatment manifested four personalities, brain wave measurements showed each had a distinct pattern of brain function. After her successful treatment, the remaining pattern was different from any one of the previous four.

Dr. Richard Kluft, a psychiatrist at the University of Pennsylvania examined over a hundred cases of multiple personalities and had this to say: (1985 ISSMP&D Conference)

'On the average there are from eight to thirteen personalities in a typical patient, although there can be more than sixty. The five most common types of personalities are: (1) the 'host' personality, typically the one who comes in for treatment; (2) a fearful, childlike personality; (3) a competent protector; (4) an 'inner prosecutor,' usually modeled after an abusive person, who tries to harm the other personalities; and (5) an 'anesthetic' personalty, impervious to pain, that apparently arose to endure abuse.'

'A multiple personality may mimic the gamut of psychiatric syndromes,' according to a report in the *Journal of Clinical Psychiatry*. It is therefore often misdiagnosed. Depending on the personality involved, the diagnoses can range from schizophrenia, severe depression to epilepsy. The report urges clinicians treating patients who have failed to respond to standard treatments to consider the possibility of multiple personality. The following controversial case presented on television is descriptive of this phenomena.

A LANDMARK TRIAL

CBS Television Network aired the program, *60 Minutes,* on Sunday, April 14, 1985. The popular program, viewed by perhaps 50,000,000 persons, presented the documentary *MPD* produced by Ira D. Rosen. CBS News Correspondent Mike Wallace conducted the interviews on two widely publicized cases of multiple personalities. One case presented here is quoted in part from the broadcast.

Mike Wallace introduced the subject. 'A man bludgeons his wife to death, but his case never goes before the jury because four psychiatrists and the judge ruled that another personality inside the man committed the murder. The man suffers from MPD, Multiple Personality Disorder, and that can be a solid defense against charges of rape, theft or murder. MPD is a disorder in which several separate personalities exist within one brain, one body. Any one of those personalities can be in control at a particular time. Before 1979, there were only 200 cases of MPD in psychiatric literature, but in the past six years more than 2,000 cases have been found in the U.S. and many experts are convinced the illness is a great deal more common than generally believed. Of course, not all multiples are criminals; only a small percentage have such tendencies.' Wallace added that most MPD sufferers were severely abused as children.

There are numerous cases in which a person commits an act of violence, or even murder, then later cannot justify his action either to himself or others. He simply will say that he didn't know what came over his, that he had absolutely no control of his actions. When it can be substantiated that such a person is a victim of multiple personality disorder (MPD), or spirit possession, it introduces an interesting legal problem. The following controversial case was presented on the CBS program.

Wallace presented the case of Paul Miskomen, devout born-again Christian, who on the night of August 13th 1979 bludgeoned his wife, Bonnie, to death. He did not know why, he simple could not stop himself.

When Miskomen was examined by psychiatrists under the influence of sodium amytal, truth serum, and under hypnosis, the doctors made a startling discovery. Within Miskomen there was a totally different personality, one who even had a different name, Jack Kelly.

Kelly, the psychiatrists discovered, was a new personality entirely different from the mild mannered, Paul Miskomen. Kelly liked to gamble, fight, chase women and was a heavy drinker.

Occasionally when Miskomen had bouts of amnesia, Kelly took over. Kelly readily admitted not liking Paul's wife, Bonnie, and confessed killing her.

Wallace introduced Dr. Ralph Allison as one of the country's leading expert on Multiple Personality Disorders. He had examined Miskomen and testified as to his two personalities. He determined that one personality was the primary one, the other the killer.

Dr. Allison believed that a disruptive spirit by the name of Kelly had possessed Miskomen. He further stated that 40 percent of the American population believe in the possibility of spirit possession. He did not bring up such a diagnosis in court and when asked why not, replied, 'I'm not stupid.'

California Superior Court Judge Sheldon Grossfield found Paul Miskomen not guilty by reason of insanity. He ordered him to a state mental hospital where he remained for 14 month and then was released.

It is conceivable that an abused child who had been beaten into unconsciousness, could become spirit possessed. When the physical body becomes low in vital energy and a traumatic circumstance exists, the conditions are right for a takeover by an intruding spirit entity. From the data presented, this did not appear the cause of Miskomen's mental problem.

The comments made by the viewing public were generally negative. In most cases there was disbelief expressed that possession exists and that the program should use its time more advantageously. Dr. Allison's comment was to the point when he declared, 'I'm not stupid.' Obviously he was very much aware of public opinion and wished to avoid the controversy sure to develop by an eminent psychiatrist openly declaring the validity of spirit possession.

With the exception of a few doctors of psychiatry and psychology, the majority in the medical profession believe a multiple personality is simply a different expression of a single personality. In general, their treatment is to integrate the different personalities into a single personality. They reject the possibility that spirits of dead persons could be other personalities. .

ALLERGIC DISEASES CAUSED BY POSSESSION

Speaking of allergic symptoms, Dr. C.W.M. Wilson, M.D. warns 'If possessing Alien Intelligent Entities (AIEs) are responsible for the symptoms, depossession of the patient is essential. If fusion of the patient's personality with that of the possessing entities is performed under hypnosis, serious and permanent adverse psychological, and allergic side effects often follow the misdirected therapy, '(*Alternative Medicine*, Vol. 2, Nos. 3/4)

There are essentially two viewpoints. One advocates the theory that there is a single entity, the physical person being treated. The view advocated in this book is that there is one or more alien intelligent entity occupying the mind and body of the patient.

In the following chapters, I shall examine in considerable detail the concept of multiple personalities. With some exceptions, I maintain that the symptoms are identical with spirit possession. An exorcism removes the additional personalities and returns the subject to his basic single personality.

Perhaps one of the reasons that the medical people have difficulty in comprehending the reality of spirit possession is the language that is required to talk about it. This specialize vocabulary is defined in the next chapter

CHAPTER 3

Language of This World and That

As we are dealing with the invisible side of the human experience, we must work in a field of endeavor that cannot be perfectly defined. Our relationship to the spirit world is not an exact science. Many of the hypotheses cannot be proved. But they are of such practicality that by using them, sometimes startling results can be achieved. As 'toe-holds' to this inexact science, the following terminology is defined.

CONSCIOUS MIND

The conscious mind is that portion of the mind, not the brain, which weighs the inputs and facts available to make decisions.

The input to the conscious mind is from the five physical senses: seeing, hearing, touching, smelling and taste. This condition is what we think of as being in the waking state. It deals with the physical world. It is the part of the mind which does the thinking, reasoning, doubting, guessing, evaluating and judging. Most important, the conscious mind is the decision maker.

What is difficult for most persons to understand is that the conscious mind does not create. No amount of worldly input can trigger the conscious mind to come up with new ideas. We all know well educated persons who simply cannot create.

When they are placed in positions of research they fail to produce new products or innovated ideas. Regardless of their scholastic degrees, such persons are not using their inner world of consciousness where all creative ideas originate. This world is the imaginative side of our mind, the subconscious mind.

SUBCONSCIOUS MIND

The subconscious mind is also known as the subjective or the unconscious. This is the area of the mind where all emotions and feelings reside.

Within the subconscious mind are love, peace, loyalty, joy, patriotism, appreciation of art and music, anger, hatred and greed, to name a few. Also, it is where all memory resides. It is said that the subconscious remembers everything. Under hypnosis a subject can recall complete conversations made years earlier. The subconscious cannot make decisions but the feelings residing there do much to influence the decision making process. Often this state of mind is likened to daydreaming.

The conscious mind governs the subconscious. Whatever the input into the subconscious, whether right or wrong, the subconscious will act upon it. To effectively direct the subconscious in the right direction, great care must be taken to clarify the precise course of action the subconscious must take. This is forcefully done with the powerful tool of visualization.

Metaphysicians know that if you, with belief, visualize something in your mind as happening right now, the event will manifest itself. Our beliefs govern what happens to us. If our beliefs are negative in nature, we can expect our experiences to reflect the general disaster we anticipated. Should we desire to improve our lot, we must change those beliefs. Visualization of desirable conditions and events in our life will vastly improve the quality of life we will experience. This must be done with determination and purpose. Our subconscious taps the ultimate Source of Power where all our good originates.

The subconscious mind is our conduit to the Superconscious Mind. It is the gateway to a better life, to loving experiences, to vigorous health, to an abundant prosperity, and to all that makes life on this earth worth while.

The subconscious mind plays a dual role. It acts as a communication center. When requests for information, guidance or help is made by the conscious mind, that request is channeled through the subconscious to the Superconscious Mind. The fulfillment of that request comes into being from the Superconscious, back to the subconscious and on to the conscious. When that happens, we call it reality. This path is fixed. Very few of us can consciously go direct to the Superconscious. This may occur once in a lifetime and when it happens, the phenomena has been described as 'being in the light', a state of mind where a person is one with the Superconscious. Refer to Figure 1.

THE RELATIONSHIP BETWEEN THE THREE PARTS OF THE MIND

Communication normally flows from A to B to C and the reverse from C to B to A.

Only under extraordinary circumstances, communication flows directly from A to C or from C to A.

Although it may appear that the 3 parts of the Mind are separate, in reality there is no separation, but complete Unity.

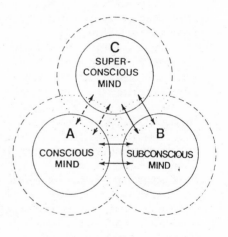

FIGURE 1

SUPERCONSCIOUS MIND

The Superconscious Mind is that part of one's mind which possesses infinite intelligence and all creative power, available everywhere all the time.

Albert Einstein (1879-1955), physicist, described the Superconscious Mind "as the ultimate formula of all that exists." It has been called the Cosmic Intelligence that governs all things. It is said to be the prime source of all that comes into being. What is most important to understand is that under the right circumstance the intelligence and power are available to you and to all human beings.

No one, to my knowledge, has proved that the Superconscious exists. As a practical matter, the supposition is that it does exist as it can be effectively used. An analogy is electricity, an unknown phenomena, but nevertheless put to practical use. Each time we direct our subconscious to reveal to us truth, to produce a miracle, or simply find a parking space for our car, we are tapping the Superconscious.

There are many excellent treatises dealing with the parts of the mind. The metaphysical book, *Science of Mind* by Ernest Holmes is one of the best on this subject.

In this work, via the pendulum and our subconscious, we communicate with the Superconscious to detect possession. As everything is known in the Superconscious, the source of our information is infinite.

Refer to Figure 1. The chart shows the path that the mind takes in requesting and receiving information. Other than in rare cases, information is channeled through the subconscious, not from the Superconscious direct to the conscious mind.

SPIRIT

The Spirit is also known as the Soul

Our spirit is you or me with or without a physical body. More commonly, the term 'spirit' is applied to a nonphysical person. Without an earthly body, the spirit has all the conscious, subconscious and superconscious elements of life. However, such spirits are powerless to function, in most instances, on the earth plane. With the proper guidance, they can progress in learning and spiritual development as they did when in the physical body. There is much truth to the saying, "As above so it is below."

In C.W. Leadbeater's book, *The Astral Plane,* on page sixty, he takes a swipe at a popular concept that we all become angels when we die. He writes:

"The poetic idea of death as a universal leveler is a mere absurdity born of ignorance. As a matter of fact, on the vast majority of cases the loss of the physical body makes no difference whatever in the character or intellect of the person.

There are therefore as many different varieties of intelligence among those whom we usually call the dead as among the living."

EARTHBOUND SPIRIT

An earthbound spirit is also known as a disembodied spirit entity, or disincarnated spirit.
These spirits know of no other place, plane or realm other than Earth. They are stuck here. Often they do not know they are dead. As a consequence, the existence such earthbound spirits lead is confusing. Usually they experience that kind of life they expected to have after dying.

Persons who believed that there would be nothing but darkness and complete oblivion after death, often find themselves in darkness without direction. They are wanderers with no place to rest. Some earthbound entities will seek a location comfortable to them. It may be a familiar home, their church, their business office or favorite bar. *My findings are that one in three homes located in an old community have one or more spirit entities in residence.* They usually cause no problem. They simply like it there.

Almost all earthbound spirit entities have no useful purpose when remaining on this plane. Most stay here because they know of no better place to go. Their presence here delays their spiritual and intellectual growth. Those of us, who practice the process of exorcism described in this book, can immeasurably help the spirit people who are lost. We can give them instruction and direct them to a higher plane of existence. This process, whether by an exorcism or by some other method, is called *rescue work*. More details on rescue work is given in Chapter 12.

POSSESSING SPIRIT ENTITY

A Possessing Spirit is an earthbound spirit, usually of low morality but often of high intelligence. He resides in the lower astral plane. Such a spirit had the opportunity and knowledge to penetrate the mind of a living person. This entity will use every wile to control the activity of his host. This spirit is the troublemaker and the one who must be thrown out of residency. An exorcism does just that. In his book, *The Dead*

Are Alive on page 111, P. Kaluaratchi explains:

"As long as an earthbound spirit remains in a disturbed, confused state of mind, he will have a feeling of hatred and other destructive thoughts toward his enemies and others he has not liked for one reason or another. If these feelings are removed, his state of mind changes. He no longer harbors ill will toward even the person who may have killed him or done him harm.

" On the other hand, we have come across malicious earthbound spirits who have influenced living persons to kill others. The persons who can be influenced in this manner are often those who can be aroused emotionally, are strong willed, and act on impulse. In this way, lower spirits can do bad deeds to those still living on earth."

Dr. Nandor Fodor defines possession: "An invasion of the living by a disincarnated spirit, tending to a complete displacement of the normal personality for the purpose of selfish gratification by the spirit."

An exorcist has a profound influence in directing an entity in the spirit world. For every possessed person the exorcist helps on this earth plane, there are usually ten or more spirits sent to a better life in their world.

I often think of an invading spirit entity as a drowning person, desperately clinging to another for help. Usually such a spirit is not vicious. It is a matter of self preservation for him. When living on earth he was never given directions or an indication what he would find after dying. He may think that possessing a living person is his sole option. He knows of no other place to go.

In general, a possessing entity is in a low spiritual state of mind and can only bring harm to the invaded host body. It follows that a more advanced spirit entity would not want to return to the earth plane to gratify some physical yearning. He would, therefore, be least likely to possess a living person.

TELEPATHY

Whether we are aware of it or not, we are always communicating with persons in our immediate vicinity. When we are conversing with a person face to face, we are often aware of the other's thoughts, even before those thoughts are expressed. Also, very often we are sending thoughts to distant places and receiving them as well. This phenomenon is known as Telepathy. Dr.J.B. Rhine of Duke University, pioneer investigator in psychic phenomena, conducted extensive experiments on thought transference. These tests were documented by the *Scientific American Magazine* as early as 1932. A decade later in 1942, Dr. Rhine published his findings in his celebrated book, *New Frontiers of the Mind.*

During the early period of Dr. Rhine's experiments in telepathy, another scientist, Harold Sherman, conducted his pioneering experiment in long distance telepathic impressions from the Arctic explorer, Sir Hubert Wilkins, during his Arctic expedition. On August 1937, Sir Hubert had been commissioned by the Soviet government to look for Sigismund Levanevsky and five companions. They had disappeared on a flight to trail blaze a polar air route from Russia to the United States. *Thoughts Through Space* by Sherman and Sir Hubert is the account of that search and is a testimony to the accuracy and reality of telepathy.

At a distance of hundreds of miles, Sherman was often able to record the daily experiences of Sir Hubert. On one occasion he accurately reported his friend flying "low over shaggy white and shadowy peaks." On this flight Sherman had the correct impression that Sir Hubert had a map of some kind on which he marked and kept some sort of record. On another occasion, Sherman recorded his impression that there had been some work done to the rear of a plane. In both instances the events were confirmed.

WATCH THOSE THOUGHTS!

The relationship we have with another person is often fixed soon after the first meeting. How we feel about a person is usually irrationally determined by our prejudices. We ask ourselves: Does he have the kind of face I like? Is he fat, skinny or just right? Is he too old or too young? How do I feel about the color of his skin? How is he dressed? Do I like the way he talks? All your observations and much more, produce an instant evaluation. You either like the person, are neutral, or don't like him.

Whatever your conclusions are of the other person, he has subconsciously picked up your thoughts. He knows how you feel. As a consequence of your thoughts, his opinion of you is also fixed. In a few seconds you have made a friend or antagonist. I well recall the incident which first made me aware of the reality of telepathy.

In 1973 I visited the psychic surgeons of the Philippines. Harold Sherman in his book, *Wonder Healers of the Philippines*, describes how these healers use bare hands to perform physical surgical operations without instruments. Such operations strain the credulity of Americans witnessing it. I became well acquainted with a family of healers.

One day while conversing with a young Philippino healer, I began a statement, "I have a problem." Before I could continue, he said, "Yes, I know." He then gave me an accurate description of the problem I was about to describe. I had given him no hint of what was on my mind. From that moment on, I was careful to have only positive thoughts when around the healers. I was rather amused by another more recent experience.

Ann, a successful young lady who was the top IBM sales person in the Chicago area expressed a concern to me. "Mr. Maurey," she said, "Even though I do well in sales, I occasionally meet some very nasty people. What can I do?"

I smiled and replied, "No problem, Ann; here is what you do." Then I outlined the steps she should take. "Before calling on a sales prospect, say to yourself, He is an Okay person, I like this person, he likes me." I explained to her that her attitude toward her prospective customer determines the relationship she will have with him.

Two days later an enthusiastic saleslady phoned me. "It works!" She exclaimed, "There is this buyer who always goes out of her way to be nasty to me. This time I really gave her cause to berate me. She started on me. Abruptly, she changed her tone and said, 'That's all right, Ann, anyone can make a mistake.' Later that same afternoon a similar experience occurred."

Telepathy is as real in the spirit world as it is in ours. A spirit entity communicates by thought transference. Our thoughts are a strong attraction in drawing a spirit to us. When we think about a person who has died, we frequently establish direct contact with that person. Most of the time we are unaware of the person's presence. If we continually think about a particular deceased person, we could inadvertently draw that person within our mind. Often this is how a possession starts.

CLAIRVOYANCE

Clairvoyance is defined as the faculty of discerning objects not visible to the physical senses. The word is derived from the French, meaning clear vision. It does not refer to the ordinary physical senses, but rather to a supernormal sense perception. As such visions do not enter our minds through the physical senses where then is their origin? They come from the subconscious level of mind. Saying it in another way, communications are carried out by the involuntary nervous system working through the machinery of the subconscious mind.

When clairvoyance is used in the diagnosis of disease it is often called X-ray vision. The course offered by *Silva Mind Control*, designed by Jose Silva, teaches one to develop clairvoyance for the purpose of pinpointing areas of disease. The term third-eye, referred to in Eastern cultures, is analogous to clairvoyance. The Philippino healers have developed their third eye to a level of a sixth sense. My visit with the Philippino psychic surgeons gave startling examples of X-ray vision.

As I observed the psychic healer, David Elizalde, he seemed to look into the body of his patient. His eyes were open yet his whole demeanor was relaxed and far away. After he had made his analysis, he turned to his brother, Louis, and asked,

"Do you see it too?" His finger pointed to a spot on his patient.

"Yes," Replied Louis, "The tumor is two inches below your finger."

At another time, while walking on a street near my hotel in Manila, the well known healer, Alex Orbito, passed me and pointed to my chest. "I can fix that," he said. He was referring to a problem I had with my heart.

Anyone can learn the art of clairvoyance with practice. One method is to sit in a comfortable chair, close your eyes and relax. It is inadvisable to cross your legs or have your clothing too tight. Pressure on your body and poor blood circulation can cause your concentration to become distracted. Relaxation usually can be quickly achieved by deep breathing. After three or four deep and slow breaths, direct your mind to the place, time or situation about which you desire more information. Whatever pictures or feelings you may have in this state of mind - called the 'alpha state' - will usually have a direct connection with the information you are seeking. At first you may have difficulty in believing the reliability of the information. As you practice this art you will become more confident in its validity and usefulness.

The faculty of clairvoyance is not absolutely essential when working in the spirit world. It is convenient at times to 'see' what is happening to make evaluations of a spirit's circumstance. Many persons with their third eye have the psychic ability to see ghosts or apparitions using normal eye sight. Because those who have this ability cannot turn it on or off at will, it is usually difficult to prove. I take the point of view that if something is useful, use it. Let someone else try to prove it.

CLAIRAUDIENCE

The ability to hear a voice originating in the subconscious is clairaudience. This is much like clairvoyance; instead of a picture, it is an extension of ordinary physical hearing. The faculty of 'hearing' is developed by lowering the brain waves into the alpha range and simply 'listening' for the answers. This cultivated gift is useful when questioning a spirit entity to determine his point of view and reactions to your explanations, arguments or directions. In later chapters I demonstrate clairaudience to facilitate the clearing process.

To understand the other side we need to explore what goes on there. An analogy would be traveling to a foreign land and examining the customs and actions of its inhabitants. The thoughts of the people would certainly interest us. We would be aware of their clothing if it differed markedly from ours. We would also wish to view the landscape, the buildings and the vegetation. We could outline their pattern of life; we may interpret it into rules or laws of conduct. This is the approach used in the next chapter to determine the laws of the other side.

CHAPTER 4

Laws of the Nonphysical World

Since we are dealing with non-tangible spirit entities, we must acknowledge that we are dealing with the spirit world. Every action we take, therefore, must be consistent with the laws of that world. Because of the universal nature of the spirit world, we have great latitude to function in a selective and immediate intercourse with any spirit or ambiguous part of that world. When we realize the extent of the spirit world and understand, at least partially, the reality of that world, we can effectively function there and produce results that can be measured. Such results are not miracles but simply the working of little known laws. C.W. Leadbeater, in his book, *The Astral Plane*, bluntly states his views on the spirit world . (p.3)

"The first point which it is necessary to make clear in describing this astral plane is its absolute reality. In using the word in its plain, everyday sense, I mean by it that the subjects and inhabitants of the astral plane are real in exactly the same way as our own bodies, our furniture, our houses or monuments are real - as real as Charing Cross to quote an expressive remark from one of the earliest Theosophical works." (Charing Cross is a railroad station at the Strand of London, England).

Dr. Michael Harner, Ph.D., Shaman and founder of the center for Shamanic Studies in Connecticut, describes the "Great Beyond" as follows:

"When one is in the non-ordinary reality, things will seem quite as material as they are here. One feels the coldness or warmth of the air, the hardness or smoothness of a rock; one perceives colors, sounds, odors, and so forth. All the phenomena that characterize the so-called material world will appear just as real and material there as they do here."

When dealing with the spirit world or the other side. the following laws are applicable. These are practical working tools useful in understanding that other world. They should be accepted and used even when the physical senses give no immediate evidence that they are working.

1. CON ARTIST OR FRIEND?

When a spirit entity communicates with a living person, the thoughts of the entity can influence that person . If the entity is of good character, the person may have something to gain. On the other hand, should the entity be of low morality and resort to cunning, the person making the contact may be in considerable danger. The identity given may not be correct. It may well be a false name given to mislead the person. The impostor may try to palm himself off as a long forgotten uncle, a grandparent dead for many years or a person not too readily identifiable. For the gullible, the entity may even declare he is a "Master" or a "Prophet"! This often happens when the ouija board is used. Great care, therefore, is advisable when interviewing a spirit entity. Skepticism is the order of the day.

An amusing incident occurred during a seance I attended. The trance medium contacted a spirit who identified himself as none other than the great Saint Francis. I questioned the "saint" on a few fundamentals of metaphysics and spiritual healing. His answers were evasive and showed a lack of knowledge of such subjects. He was a masquerador. I had asked myself, "Why would a saint play parlor games with a small group of people?"

2. COMMUNICATION

We of the living world have trouble in receiving communication from the other side. It is difficult to quiet our minds and listen to what is being said. We are involved with our personal affairs and the external distractions about us. In the spirit world there is no such limitation.

A living person can communicate with most spirits on the other side by speaking his name or simply thinking about him! When making such a contact, the spirit usually presents himself. A face-to-face conversation can take place. Some psychics claim to 'see' the spirits when they appear.

There have been many spirit-written books by mediums who channel information from the other side. A few are *Arthur Ford Speaks* written by Eileen Sullivan, *Philosophy of Silver Birch* edited by Stella Storm, *As We See It From Here* compiled by the Holmes Research Team, and the well known book, *Seth Speaks* by Jane Roberts. These books were written by various methods. Silver Birch's messages came through Maurice Barbanell, trance medium and editor of Psychic News. Arthur Ford's work was typed by the sensitive, Eileen Sullivan. George Meek, parapsychologist, and his associates supervised and edited the research on the life of Dr. Jesse Holmes. Dr Holmes's message came at different times through several trance mediums.

Should one desire to talk to the spirit of a dead person, it is not difficult to do so. Arthur Ford suggested a simple method to communicate with the dead. It is the method I use. Following his suggestion, I relax in a comfortable chair at my desk with pad and pencil. I then address the entity I wish to talk to by first writing out a greeting to the individual. Then I proceed to ask questions. All questions and answers are recorded. I have developed a clairaudience ability which one can easily learn - to listen' to the answers the spirit person gives me. Often, if I know the spirit to whom I am 'talking', I can actually recognize the voice of the speaker. To record the information more easily, a tape recorder or typewriter can be used.

THE TROUBLEMAKER

The following is a typical conversation with a spirit who had been causing trouble to Kevin, a young man, age twenty-five. Kevin proclaimed he loved drinking and had no intention of giving it up. This case was brought to me by Kevin's aunt. At my request, she provided me with names of some of her close dead relatives. It was possible that one was the possessing spirit. It developed that the aunt's brother, Daniel, was a likely candidate. I determined to talk to him. With pad and pencil I recorded the following conversation. (The names have been changed to insure privacy.)

Rev. M. "I would like to talk to Daniel Bell, brother of Madeleine Bell." I paused a moment and then pointed to a nearby chair. "Please be seated. Are you aware you are dead?"

Daniel. "No, I'm not dead."

Rev. M. "In a way you are correct. You feel very much alive, but you are not of this earth plane."

Daniel. "What do you mean?"

Rev. M. "You see, dying is like going through a doorway into another room. But staying here, you are causing trouble both to yourself and Kevin."

Daniel. "That's nonsense. Why should I hurt Kevin? I can only do him some good."

Rev. M. "Are you aware that Kevin has become an alcoholic such as you were when you lived here?"

Daniel. "Yes, what of it!"

Apparently, the conversation was getting nowhere, as the possessing spirit residing in Kevin had little conscience nor wished to mend his ways. I therefore decided to start the exorcism.

Rev. M. "Let me explain something to you. First of all, you do not belong here on this plane. You belong in a far better place. Let me introduce you to a friend and guide whom you know and trust." The guide then became visible to Daniel. "Your friend will now escort you to your next level of development and truth where your every need will be supplied. Above all, you will be with your friends and loved ones who are on the same side of the curtain of death as you are."

Rev. M. "What do you think about all this?"

Daniel: "It may be a good idea."

Rev. M. Taking a deep breath, I fairly shouted, "Then I bid you go!" Clairvoyantly, I noted that the spirit, Daniel, did not look back but his friend did and said, "Thanks!" Kevin was now free from the influence of the alcoholic Daniel.

PAPA KNOWS BEST

In another interesting case, I had discovered the subject's father was the possessing entity. Even though a person is dead there is ample evidence he still has self will. All too often it is directed in the wrong direction.

Rev. M. "I would like to talk to Mr. W., father of Aaron. Would you please be seated in that chair." I indicated a nearby chair.

Rev.M "Are you near your son, Aaron?"

Mr. W. "Yes, I am."

Rev M. "Why?"

Mr. W. "Because he needs me and I know what's best for him.

Rev.M. "Let me tell you what type of trouble you are bringing him. Any disease you had, he can now have. You are interfering with both his mental and spiritual growth. This you may not do. What is your comment?"

Mr. W. "I don't care. I still think it is the best thing to do."

Rev.M. "Let me give you an insight into "your new life."

It serves no purpose to argue with a spirit. At this point I performed an exorcism, modifying it to suit the situation. I believe he was slightly incredulous when he left. Either he did not know that he was dead or had no belief in an afterlife. He obviously was a stubborn person. There is no absolute certainty the possessing spirit was the father. Nevertheless, the intruding spirit was sent on his way thereby clearing Aaron.

3. DIRECTING A SPIRIT

When speaking with a positive and sincere tone of voice, a living person may give suggestions or direct orders to a disembodied spirit. Usually The spirit will accept them. As such statements may greatly affect the 'life' of the entity, some knowledge about his world is essential.

During a clearing of entities it is wise to be persuasive when describing the plane of development where the entity should go. In the astral plane as on Earth, far more can be attained by using sugar than vinegar. As a rule, one is dealing with confused and lost souls. Kindness and understanding of their unfortunate state of mind is recommended. It isn't often the exorcist can get an immediate confirmation that his approach is correct. The following case gives an unusual twist to the departure of a cooperative spirit entity.

THE EAVESDROPPER

Camille K. was a developed natural sensitive, yet had little control over this ability. She had not learned to turn her psychic talent on or off at will. She was the clearinghouse for any stray spirit entity who wished to talk to her. Day and night she had to listen to their talk, most of which was nonsense. She even resorted to answering them. She got little sleep, becoming so desparate that she was close to a nervous breakdown. As her case was obviously one of possession, an associate and knowledgeable healer, Rev. Gerald Loe, referred her to me. I immediately went to work and cleared away most of the entities. Shortly afterwards she informed me by phone that some of the stronger ones remained. Continuing my efforts, they proved to be more difficult to throw out but eventually they also left. A week later, I phoned Camille to ask her if all was well.

Camille. "Yes, it is much more peaceful now, except for a soft speaking spirit who appears friendly. He is talking to me now."

Rev. M. "What is he saying?"

Camille. "He says, 'Listen to him; he can help you; he is telling you the truth.'

Rev. M. "You mean to tell me he can hear me when I speak to you?"

Camille. "Oh yes, he hears every word."

Obviously, this spirit wasn't a bad sort of fellow. I decided to risk talking directly to him with the objective of sending him on his way.

Rev. M. "Let me talk to him. Remember, I'm talking to him, not to you, Camille."

Camille. "I understand."

Rev. M. "Let me explain to you where and who you are. You are dead yet feel very much alive. This is perfectly natural. You do not belong on this earth plane, you belong in a far better place. Let me introduce you to a friend whom you know and trust, and who is nearby you now. This friend will now take you to your next plane of development where you will receive healing, help and guidance; where your every need will be supplied. You will be with those you love and those who love you."

Camille. "(Laughing) He's going. He said goodbye!"

4. CREATING AN ENVIRONMEMT

A person can create any condition whatsoever for a spirit by simply visualizing it or by verbally describing it. A place, another spirit person or a situation can thus become reality for the entity. As thoughts are things in the spirit world, the spirit person, for example, can also create for himself the environment, the house he lives in, and the persons with whom he associates.

In the clearing process, it is useful to introduce the invading spirit entity to an advanced spirit, often called a spirit guide. A guide is always available and willing to help. If the entity can be convinced his situation will improve, he becomes more willing to leave.

THE STICKY GUEST

Those in the medical profession who define a multiple personality as an invasion of one or more spirit entities, often use hypnotism to talk to the spirits.

Dr. Edith Fiori, a psychologist practicing in California, hypnotizes her patients to contact a possessing entity. Under hypnosis, the entity can speak using the voice box of the patient. In one very difficult and prolonged case she could not get the entity to leave. The intruder had been a Roman Catholic when alive. Because of the immoral life he had lived, he believed he would go to hell when he died. He was convinced that was his next stop and he wasn't about to leave the comfort and safety of the host body.

After several months of futile discussion with the stubborn spirit, the doctor hit upon a unique solution. She asked for a spirit Catholic priest to help the possessing spirit! A priest immediately appeared and became visible to the obstinate spirit. The priest assured him that he would not go to hell. On the contrary, he would live in a very attractive place of peace and love. The reluctant one left with the priest. The patient was cleared.

5. LANGUAGE NO PROBLEM

Spirit people do not speak in their world; they communicate via telepathic thought. Such thought must of necessity be truthful as it is not possible for spirits to hide their thoughts from each other. Since there are no spoken words, differences in languages are not a problem.

An English soldier who had died long after the ending of World War I, told his story through the English medium,

Leslie Flint. The ex-soldier was not earthbound and had strongly resisted returning to earthly affairs and people. He had a good deal and wanted to keep it. In his travels on the other side he told the following story.

As a disembodied spirit the soldier returned to a farm house in France where the French farmers had been most kind to him during the war. In particular, there had been an attractive young lady there whom he was anxious to see again. Although he recalled that the farm building had been destroyed during the war and the occupants killed, he was surprised to find the house as it once was. His old friends were there, alive and warmly welcomed him. During his former wartime visits he had a language difficulty when communicating with the French people. Now he found he could easily converse with his old friends.

6. WHAT DO WE BELIEVE?

In the spirit world, it also follows that the conditions surrounding the entity are influenced by his thinking. This offers the potential for the entity to create an environment pleasing to him. His thoughts and desires are expressed in visible form. He may create for himself an ideal home, a pleasant village or city; he can attract friends with whom to converse or find a teacher to further his enlightenment.

There is no reward or punishment in that other realm but only the actual result of what the man himself has done and said and thought while here on earth. In fact, the man makes his bed during earth life, and afterwards has to lie on it.

The beliefs a person has while living have much to do with what he expects when he dies. Should he expect the end of all things and the termination of his soul into nothingness, he may find himself lost in darkness. At best, he may have no place to go or rest. Spirit persons in this category make up the vast majority who remain earthbound. These are the so called ghosts, apparitions and poltergeists. They are badly in need of direction and help.

Often a soldier killed on a battlefield will try as a disembodied spirit to continue fighting. Often he does not know at first that he is dead, and he also may not believe in an afterlife. He may still have the same hatred for the enemy that he had just previous to dying. He may still feel the pain of his fatal wound. Such spirits have a difficult time reconciling themselves to their new environment.

7. SPIRIT ENERGIES

When something needs to be done in the living world, it takes the thought and energy of a living person to do it. Those in the spirit world do not have the ability or energy to accomplish tasks in the physical world. They cannot perform any physical activity unless they utilize in some way the physical energy of a living person or animal. For further insight into how human energy is used by a possessing spirit, I present the following amusing story.

CASE OF THE DOCTOR'S GHOST

This is a true story related to me by Bill and Eleanor Guennewig of Belville, Illinois, two sober and no-nonsense people. A psychic friend mentioned to them that she had observed colored lights in a corner of a chiropractor's office. She had interpreted the lights as a ghost. Eleanor, intrigued by meeting a real live ghost, decided to investigate the doctor's office with the prospect of exorcising the ghost. She had heard of such work being done and being a dowser felt up to the task. She would have been safer joining the Marines for a six-year hitch! This is her story:

"Upon entering the room at the doctor's office which reportedly housed the ghost, I pointed my dowsing L-rods at the corner where the intruder was said to be and commanded; 'You get out of here!'

"Without warning, invisible hands snatched the L-rods from my hands and a powerful force threw me to the floor! I had to crawl out of the room on my hands and knees. I was shocked and could not believe what had happened to me.

"After awhile, with more courage than wisdom, I went back to try again. Act II was a repeat performance of Act I. Again, I was thrown to the floor by an invisible force - I felt no hands. I retreated on hands and knees. it was then I made up my mind this was not my kind of work, it was a job for a professional. I contacted you, Rev. Maurey."

For me the clearing at a distance of the doctor's office was routine, of no special significance . The spirit readily left .

It was only later that I learned the full story of the battle between the sexes (the ghost evidently hated women). The doctor reported feeling more comfortable in his office, but could not explain why.

The ghost or poltergeist apparently liked the doctor. The doctor did not even know he was there. Since a spirit entity normally has no physical energy, he can on occasion absorb the excess energy from a small child or animal. In this case, he had accumulated the energy thrown off during the manipulations by the chiropractor.

This example gives more credibility to the advice: Do the clearing in the safety of your home, away from the possessed person or haunted house. It's effective and besides it's nonhazardous to both your body and dignity.

As an indication of how this energy may be accumulated, I recently attended a high school reunion held in a private dining room connected to a large popular ball room. There were about 200 persons in attendance at the reunion and another 200 to 300 couples on the dance floor. At the conclusion of the reunion I felt good. In fact, I had so much energy I had considerable difficulty in going to sleep that evening. It was only after reading three nonfictional books, that I was tired enough to get two hours sleep.

The size of the aura that a person has is indicative of the total physical energy the person has. The larger the aura the greater the energy. As the energy is used, it diminishes in size. Psychic energy, such as described in the above story, is accumulated in the aura. Likewise, a spirit has an energy field which when fully energized can he felt and often seen. Spirits accumulate psychic energy in very much the same way as I did at the reunion. When they are in the presence of such energy, they can draw upon it to produce poltergeist activities or use it for a more useful purpose. The aura is discussed in detail in Chap. 6.

ARE SPIRITS REAL?

A spirit entity often is not aware of other spirits nearby. It is quite possible for two or more entities to occupy the same physical space at the same time.

There is a process called psychic photography in which photographs are produced of people who are dead. Such photographs often show a multitude of faces crowded around the person photographed. A photographer with a special psychic gift does this work. He usually uses an ordinary camera and film.

I am aware that often there are many spirits around an individual. Using the pendulum, I frequently count 30 or more spirits near a person. Quite a crowd for a telephone booth!

9. FREEDOM BY DYING

A spirit who is not of this world cannot be possessed by another in his world. It therefore follows that when a possessed person dies, his spirit becomes free of the possessing spirit.

There is considerable evidence that a spirit entity can gain access to the body of a person rather easily. It is also true his exit from that body it not so easy. Very often a strong negative entity tires of the body he possesses and tries to get out by convincing his host to commit suicide or commit a crime with penalty of death. My records are full of such cases of persons who when possessed committed crimes or who contemplated suicide.

In the United States there are more than 400 recorded jail house suicides per year. Jail suicides worldwide typically occur within two hours after an arrest. Alcohol is present nearly always. "The majority of jail suicides are not suicidal people," says Lindsay Hayes, an expert at the National Center on Institutions and Alternatives, now completing his second nationwide study on the subject. "Suicide results when anxiety, guilt, and a forbidding cell environment combine with a drug that reduces your inhibitions to do things you wouldn't normally do."

10. WE DON'T DIE

When a person dies, he does not immediately become more intelligent or knowledgeable. He enters the astral plane at the same intellectual and spiritual level in which he left this world. As his learning and wisdom increases, he rises to a higher plane of enlightenment. Eventually, he will have little or nothing more to do with the astral plane or the physical world.

The spirit persons who communicate through a medium often complain that it is difficult to lower their vibrations to be able to talk. In a sense, the degree of spirituality can be equated to vibration. The more evolved a spirit entity is, the higher is his vibration. As a consequence few such spirits revisit the earth with its lower frequency. It is my personal observation that a person who has recently died has trouble in speaking through a medium. Their usual explanation is that they have not yet learned to lower their vibrations.

To better understand how vibration effects our consciousness, let's talk about our ability to see and hear. Each person has a vibrational range in which they hear. It varies, but normally it is in the range of 100 to 25,000 hertz (cycles per second). A dog and cat, however, hear in a range exceeding the human ear. A whistle producing 30,000 hertz can clearly be heard by a dog or cat, yet not be heard by the human ear.

As a personal analogy, I often heard a soft tinkling bell off somewhere to my right yet I could not locate the source there. Finally, I observed that my new wristwatch had an alarm and at a given hour it would chime. The watch was on my left wrist. It was then that I discovered that my left ear was limited to a lower frequency than the right ear.

We, as humans, can see a range of light vibrations in colors of the familiar solar spectrum from red to violet. Yet beyond this range other colors exist. There is the ultraviolet spectrum containing a multitude of color variations which can be photographed and identified. So-called white light from a star can be filtered through a special prism and its light analyzed for the minerals existing on that heavenly body. Yet to the human eye it is but a twinkling star.

Just because we cannot see something or hear it, it doesn't mean that it doesn't exist.

ELECTRONIC VOICES

Thomas Alva Edison (1847-1931), inventor of the phonograph, was one of the first to experiment with an instrument to capture voices on the other side. He did not succeed. It was one of his greatest disappointments. Persons interested in electronics have recently made remarkable progress in communicating with spirit beings. Harold Sherman's book, *The Dead Are Alive*, documents some of the work being done today.

Sherman reports the work of Friedrich Juergenson of Molbo, Sweden, who devoted four years to diligent and scientific recording of thousands of spirit voices. Not all voices came in loud and clear. Some spirit persons were able to identify themselves. In 1965, Dr. Konstantin Raudive, psychologist and author, joined Juergenson. Later, Raudive analyzed some 80,000 recordings which became the basis for his monumental book, *Breakthrough*.

SAINTS OR SINNERS?

By the very nature of a highly evolved spiritual person, there is the constant drive for greater awareness. After death such a person continues in this direction. There is no looking back to the physical attachments experienced when alive on earth.

On the other hand, an unevolved person of little spirituality, does not readily give up his attachments for material things or pleasures. Even though he is dead, he does not change. He may still crave alcoholic drink, stimulating drugs, sexual experiences, or the predilection to harm others. These are the negative spirit entities and the ones most likely to seek an acceptable host body to possess. As when living, these are the troublemakers. When a highly intelligent spirit entity is of low moral character, his capacity to do harm to his host is almost limitless.

In his book, *What Then*, George Meek, the distinguished parapsychologist, characterizes the spirit being as follows:

"It has been observed that death does not make a saint of a sinner, or a sage of a fool. The individual carries over all the old beliefs, the old habits, the old desires and all of his faulty teachings and religious dogmas. Those who believe that there is no afterlife are not at all prepared for what they find."

C.W. Leadbeater in a similar vein expresses the transition into spirit. (*The Other Side of Death*, p.130)

"The state of affairs found as actually existing is much more rational than most of the current theories. It is not found that any sudden change takes place in the man at death, or that he is spirited away to some heaven beyond the stars. On the contrary, man remains after death exactly what he was before it. He is the same in intellect, the same in his qualities and powers. The conditions into which he passes are precisely those he made for himself."

11. LIFE ON THE ASTRAL PLANE

The astral plane is that place of existence to which we go shortly after dying. It is similar to our earth but with many differences. It is described as a realm of intense and beautiful colors, as a peaceful place, and where all one's needs are supplied. It is more real than the living world we know. It is where, upon dying, we will meet those near and dear to us who have died. It is a place for learning and for greater spiritual awareness. As on earth, there are many tasks to perform there. It is no place for the lazy or idle person. Leadbeater further comments: (p. 130)

"The astral plane is one stage higher than the physical. Therefore its possibilities, both of enjoyment and of progress, are in every way greater than those of the lower level, earth. But the possibilities are themselves of a higher character, and it requires a certain amount of intelligence and good sense to take advantage of them. If a man is so undeveloped intellectually that during the physical stage of his life he has not been able to look beyond that state, but has devoted the whole of his thought and energy solely to material things, he is little likely to be able to adapt himself to more advanced conditions. Since he neglected or was too blind to see the smaller opportunities of the physical, it is scarcely probable that his half-atrophied mind will be strong enough to grasp the wider possibilities of this grander life."

On the other side there is complete freedom of choice. No one directs a spirit person (soul) against his will. There is guidance but not coercion. As the spirit person adapts himself to his new environment, he becomes more knowledgeable about how to deal with it better. As it is on the earth plane, wise decisions are based on knowledge and experience.

A spirit may create anything in his/her world by thought alone. Thought governs his environment, the home he lives in, the people he meets, the work he chooses to do. The limitations he experiences are those he places on himself. Every opportunity to expand his awareness is available to him.

Spiritual growth is synonymous with service to others. There is every opportunity to serve. A soul may work as a helper in a reception center, he may teach, he may involve himself in rescue work, or he may seek to give aid to those yet in the physical world.

On the other side a soul can continue to grow physically as well as spiritually. Should a child die, he may continue to grow up physically in that other world in much the same way he would have developed if he had lived. His parents upon their arrival to his world will often meet him as a fully grown adult.

On the other hand, an elderly person who died may appear

as a person in the prime of life. The form of appearance may be altered to conform to the expectations of a new arrival or old friend long in the spirit world.

12. NO CLOCKS

Time does not exist in the spirit world. There, all thought and action is instantaneous. For a spirit, a hundred years is equally long as a snap of a finger. This fact may explain the existence of so many confused spirits in the nonphysical world. Although they may be 'living' in our time, they actually may have died five hundred years ago in a period long forgotten and not remotely related to our present way of life.

13. HELPERS ON THE OTHER SIDE

As we are talking about the spirit world, we cannot very well ignore the possibility that there are highly evolved spiritual beings on the other side, able and willing to help us. All evidence indicate that these beings exist. Such spirits are called Guardian Angels, Friends, Guides, Counselors, or Helpers. They are volunteers serving a living person. Most persons have four or at least two highly developed spirits with them. Should a person have a need, they are available to help. A person engaged in humanitarian work may have as many as twelve. They come and go as the person's needs change.

For myself, one of my most active helpers on the other side is a spirit guide whom I call George. From my experience with working with George, I recognize his expertise and effectiveness. Even though I know it is not necessary to give detailed instructions to George, I often do, as I conscientiously do not wish to miss any opportunity to assist a misguided entity in every way possible. Rather than eject an entity out and into an unknown and perhaps fearful environment. I persuade him/her to leave voluntarily knowing he/she will be met by a helpful guide.

Should a living person desire something done on the other side, an advanced spirit is the correct channel to accomplish the task. These intermediaries are helpful in keeping us safe from real or imagined harm by elements of the spirit world. Since one is a novice at best when working in the astral plane, it is wise to let the enlightened spirits perform one's requests when it pertains to the Next Dimension.

The question has been asked: If a person is possessed by a spirit entity, why doesn't a highly evolved spirit, such as a spirit guide who certainly must be aware of the condition, take corrective action on his own volition? It has been my observation that the spirit world does not interfere with the free will of a living person. A living person must always make a request of the spirit helper. It may be that we are our brother's keeper.

During a visit to the London home of the late, well known trance mediums, Lily and George Wheatley, a spirit friend by the name of Josua introduced himself as my special 'friend'. He greeted me with the caustic comment, "I've been after you for a long time. It's about time you're doing this work!" He was referring to my healing ministry. We have had no reason to speak to each other since that first meeting.

For those persons knowledgeable in metaphysics, it should be noted that the laws and conditions described above are not too dissimilar to the laws applied to our earth life.

As we progress in this study, we shall have many occasions to use the laws of the spirit world and to verify their effectiveness by the results achieved. When the spirit personalities are no longer influencing the subject, the changes brought about are often of a miraculous nature.

It should be emphasized that I attribute none of this work to the supernatural. In general, it can be explained as a logical outcome of natural law.

The exorcist must have an understanding of the environment and situation in which the earthbound spirit finds himself. To help the spirit entity, the exorcist must have a knowledge of the laws which govern that other world. These laws are clearly defined in this chapter and are useful tools during an exorcism.

In the majority of cases a person will not know that he is spirit possessed. He will be unable to disassociate his basic personality from that of the invader. Even if his intimate friends and associates never heard of spirit possession, they will know that something is wrong with him. Why and how such a person becomes possessed is the subject of the following chapter.

CHAPTER 5
Causes of
Spirit Possession

Psychic Attack, whether it is spirit possession or comes in some other form, may happen to anyone at any time. The condition may come into being whether or not the victim has a knowledge of psychic activities. The problems may range from only a minor illness, a negative change in attitude to a complete change of personality. Unless the victim or someone near him can recognize the symptoms and seek help from a competent psychic, he is in serious trouble. With such help the psychic can unravel the causes of such infestation and correct the problem. Such help will restore the mind as well as improve the health of the patient.

There are two common roads to possession. The first is voluntarily asking a spirit to enter one's mind. In most instances the victim does not realize that he caused this condition. His motive may have been sympathy, grief, need for companionship, or simply curiosity. No evil was intended. The second is a state of mind when a spirit enters without invitation. This is called an involuntary possession. Whether a possession is voluntary or involuntary, it usually leads to serious problems for the victim as well as for those the victim influences.

When possessed, voluntary or involuntary, the person in some way attracted a spirit entity to himself by an overt action or thought. In almost every case the victim of a possession is entirely unaware that he caused the possession. Also, more frequent than not, he is not aware that he is spirit possessed.

VOLUNTARY POSSESSION

The circumstances of a voluntary possession can occur when the subject has strong feelings of endearment for another person who died. The subject may feel the dead person can still contribute to his/her life. When a living person thinks often, particularly with emotion, about a person who died, the spirit of the dead person is almost always present. Sorrow strengthens this attachment. When one grieves on this side, the other grieves on the other side. Under such circumstances, there is the danger that the spirit of the dead person can be drawn to the subject and, eventually, enter the mind of that person. Usually the subject feels comfortable with such a spirit but the decision making process and actions which follow can be very erratic. An example of a voluntary possession is illustrated in the following case.

CASE OF THE CLOSE FRIEND

Just what is it like to be possessed? How does it feel when there is another personality sharing one's mind? Dennis R. described his experience to me.

"Before my friend Milton died, I was sympathetic and understanding toward him. I always excused his rather irrational behavior as the outcome of a deprived early childhood. When I knew him, he was an alcoholic and a heavy pill user. He had pills to lift him into a high exuberant state of mind and pills to put himself to sleep. After awhile, neither type of pill was effective. All too often he mixed his pills with whiskey. It was a sure road to sudden unconsciousness for him.

"After Milton's death, the feeling of closeness was still strong. I thought this was perfectly natural. It wasn't long before I noticed that I was beginning to think like Milton in various small ways, such as the clothes I chose to wear and the type of music I would listen to. I also began to drink when I felt emotionally disturbed. Normally, I regarded myself as a solid citizen, a person to whom others go for advice. I began to question that image.

"After several years, my complete attention was no longer on my work, as it should have been. I spent increasingly more time pursuing some irrational behavior similar to that practiced by Milton when he was alive. My service business suffered and my relationship with others deteriorated. I became depressed and often felt frustrated. Nothing went right for me. My attitude was completely negative.

"It was in this state of mind that I became acquainted with the phenomenon of possession. I asked myself, "Could I be possessed." My experience did fit the pattern. I decided to use the knowledge gained by my study of spirit possession to clear myself. I didn't know of anyone who could do it for me. I evolved a plan.

"I made the assumption that Milton was near me and could hear me. Of course, I couldn't see him. Relaxing in a comfortable chair, I spoke to him, "Milton, my friend " I said, "I've kept you in my consciousness because of my concern for you and to finish some of the things you didn't complete when you were alive." After this introduction, I continued, "I can no longer be involved with your thinking and desires; you must release me and leave." I concluded with a sharp command, "Please go now!"

"Shortly after the conversation' with Milton I felt different; my old self again came into focus. The rather strange ideas I had no longer carried weight with me. I shrugged off the values and characteristics which were not mine but which most certainly had been Milton's. It was only then that I fully comprehended how deep the possession had been."

Dennis was fortunate to have been able to stop his deterioration in time to prevent complete dominance by Milton. In the final stage of possession, the subject often loses his own personality. The spirit entity, if a strong one, takes over the thinking and action of the body. When this occurs, usually after several years have elapsed, it is very difficult to dislodge the firmly entrenched entity.

When there is a single possessing entity, the entity will usually be identified as a close friend or relative. This condition occurs in about ten percent of the cases I handle. Such entities are difficult to send away permanently as the subject feels close to the intruder and will often call him/her back after the exorcism. To keep the subject clear in such cases, follow-up is necessary over a period of three to four months.

I have spoken with several persons who strongly felt they were a 'walk-in', a soul who has displaced another in a physical body. This is a complete possession where the second personality has successfully replaced the original personality and taken control of the body. Again, this may be a voluntary or involuntary action.

THE HYPOCHONDRIAC

A person whose physical illness has been medically diagnosed as imaginary, may well be a victim of possession. To further complicate such a case, a person may have several possessing spirits on board, each with different illnesses and symptoms. The medical diagnosis is different each time the victim sees a doctor. When this occurs, the patient changes doctors, going from one doctor to the next, rarely finding one who agrees with the last one.

To take on an illness of the possessing spirit is a common occurrence. A possessed person almost always suffers from ill health, some very seriously. Even a child will reflect poor health when a spirit entity becomes attached. One of the first indications of spirit possession is that usually the victim's health is less than 50 percent of the best health he has achieved during his lifetime. Usually, his 100 percent best health, occurred when he was born.

When an illness has been induced from a 'sick' spirit entity, conventional medical treatment is ineffective. Medical treatment in such cases can be compared to giving Joe an aspirin for Bill's headache. Referring to Chapter 2, Dr.Frank Putnam also noted that drugs would not consistently react predictably when two personalities were present. When the victim is cleared, there is almost always a sudden improvement in health. Over the long run there is permanent improvement.

FOREVER ILL

The next case, brought to my attention by my daughter, Robin Anderson, is a dramatic illustration of disease 'transmitted' from a spirit entity. Robin spoke to me about her friend, Karen:

"When Karen was thirteen, her mother whom she dearly loved, died. A few years afterwards her father remarried.

"Karen is now twenty-six. She hates both her stepmother and her father. Also, she has little love for her brother. She has been dreadfully ill for years and has had a series of surgical operations. I don't think she will live long. She is scheduled for another operation next week. I hope you can help her."

Although I had not met Karen, my pendulum indicated she was exhibiting the personalities of two persons, her own and of another unidentified person. Using the pendulum, I asked, "Did Karen know this person during her lifetime?" The answer was 'Yes.' "Was this person related to Karen?" Again, the answer was 'Yes.' Since there was only one spirit on board and none nearby, I began to suspect Mama was the visitor.

Further questioning indicated Karen had the same health profile her mother had six months before her death. In addition, Karen still retained a loyalty to her mother of 80 percent, unusually high for a person who had died thirteen years previously. Using the same measuring technique, I discovered that she held her father in low esteem. Finally, my pendulum indicated that the mother was the spirit on board. Karen was ever conscious of her love for her mother. At some point she could no longer distinguish her mother's personality from her own. Essentially, Karen became her mother in her thinking. It resulted in the intense hatred toward her father who had remarried and toward her father's second wife.

The solution to Karen's illness and possession was evident: Ask the mother to leave. This, I thought, should not he too difficult as the mother obviously must love her daughter and would not knowingly harm her. I proposed talking to the mother to explain the situation to her. How this can he done was described in Chapter 4, under Communication. When all was quiet in the late evening, I sat down in my favorite chair and relaxed.

Speaking aloud, I asked, "May I talk to Karen's mother?"

Assuming then that she was in my presence, I continued, "You are very close to your daughter, in fact, you now control most of her thoughts and actions. You are doing this out of love for her. She also loves you very much." Pausing, I then said with emphasis "What you don't know is that you have brought to her the disease which caused your death. She has but six months to live!" I could sense the shock that statement had on the spirit mother.

I then went on to explain what the alternatives were for the mother. With gentleness, I described where she was and the conditions under which she existed. I concluded with a description of the plane of existence where she would be reunited with friends who had also died. I introduced a guide to her who would help her in her next life of existence. With the facts explained as I knew them, I finally said to her, "It's up to you now. You can either stay with your daughter under the present circumstances or you can go with the guide." Subsequent events indicated that she left with the guide.

Karen was cleared on a Friday. On the following Monday, she canceled her scheduled operation for that week. Within a month, her health so rapidly improved that she was able to resume a more normal way of life. It was not long before she became reconciled with her father and brother and no longer hated her stepmother who had but recently died. A year after the clearing, Karen was reported to be in good health with a positive attitude. She was not told about the clearing.

ALLERGIC DISEASES

Often severe allergic symptoms can be traced to spirit possession. Dr. C.W.M. Wilson, M.D., Ph.D., Professor, Division of Geriatric Medicine, Law Hospital, Lanarkshire, Scotland, has discovered that "severe sensitivity to heavy metals (aluminum, arsenic, lead, and mercury) is characteristic of Alien Intelligent Entities (AIEs)." When depossession occurs, there is no further allergic reaction to heavy metals. This becomes the distinguishing characteristic between an AIE and an Alternative Multiple Personality (AMP). An AMP has no adverse reaction to heavy metals.

Not every exorcism results in permanent improvement. Often the subject falls victim to possession again and again. Follow up is essential to insure a constant state of freedom from interfering spirit entities. The following is such a case.

GRANDFATHER TAKES OVER

Julius K. is as close to me as a son. As a small child, parents could not have had a more even tempered and happy infant. At the age of four, there was a sudden change in personality. He became disruptive, violent toward his mother and childhood friends and would throw a temper tantrum if he did not get his own way.

Also, he appeared to be self destructive and would often bang his head on the walls. Later, as a teenager, in fits of anger, he smashed gaping holes in the door to his room.

As Julius became older, his violent disposition became fixed. I began to suspect that he may have become spirit possessed. As he strongly resented going to church, it was not feasible to haul him to a non-traditional church for an exorcism. A friend, with knowledge of the process of exorcism as practiced in her church, volunteered her services. She tried to clear the young man but after several attempts no improvements were noted. Julius now thirty, was working for our company at the time. Because of his violent temper directed at the other employees, we were finally forced to discontinue his employment. Then the unexpected happened.

Dr. Edward P. Jastram gave the keynote lecture at the American Society of Dowsers in Danville, Vermont. He spoke about how the pendulum could be used to detect possession and described a process of removing spirit entities using the mind only. This was a startling new approach to an exorcism. I immediately became excited with the possibilities for Julius.

Upon the conclusion of the lecture, I gently tapped the shoulder of the doctor's wife, Lydia Jastram. She was sitting directly in front of me! I explained the problem to the doctor's wife who summed it up, "Yes, I understand, he has a love-hate personality." That same evening, Dr. Jastram exorcised Julius of spirit possession. This was done at a distance of approximately 1000 miles, Danville, Vermont to Chicago. I was not prepared for the results.

The following day I phoned my office. Julius had been in. The superintendent was incredulous with the change which had come over him. The young man had gone about his former work place and cheerfully offered to help those whom he had completely alienated. All were puzzled with this change in attitude and could not account for it. Upon returning to Chicago and visiting with the young man, I found indeed there was a change. I listened intently for a negative remark and heard none. I gently probed his attitude toward me and about others at the factory, yet found no resentment.

Julius' separation from the company was a puzzle to him as he could not understand the reasons for his discharge. I am sure that he had been completely unaware of his behavior and could not account for the hostile attitude of his fellow employees. Even though Julius had taken a monumental step in his personality improvement, there were still several difficult years ahead for him.

After I had learned to perform exorcisms at a distance, with the pendulum I would frequently check Julius for possession.

Often, I would find a solitary negative entity present whom I would promptly send on his way. Yet, upon rechecking later, I would find an entity with the same characteristics as previously. Then came a revelation.

Julius had developed a non-malignant tumor on the left side of his brain. It was surgically removed. His grandfather also had the same type of tumor at the identical location! Throughout his life the young man had exhibited many of the personality characteristics of his grandfather.

I asked myself: Could the entity be Julius' grandfather who died when Julius was very young? The young man was displaying the same unruly disposition as his grandfather. Furthermore, his grandfather did not believe in an afterlife and would be the perfect candidate for an earthbound spirit.

Without further delay, I requested the presence of grandfather's spirit. I then explained to him what had happened to his grandson. I am certain the grandfather had no idea that he had brought his worldly disease to his grandson. After the explanation, I lovingly performed the exorcism. Something must have happened as there has been a steady improvement in Julius' personality since my talk with his grandfather.

When Julius was told what had transpired, he remarked, "I can use all the help I can get." More than likely this had been a welcomed voluntary possession.

INVOLUNTARY POSSESSION

When a person is in a state of low vitality he is exposed to possession by an intruding spirit. This can occur during a surgical operation or when unconscious while intoxicated or when seriously injured. At these times, the mind of a person is defenseless and there is insufficient energy to resist the intrusion of a strong spirit personality. This is an involuntary possession. A prolonged illness, in which the subject has long been in a state of exhaustion, can permit an entity to take over a person's mind and body. The person simply does not have the strength to ward off the intruder.

ALCOHOLISM

In our society today, there is perhaps no faster road to possession than excessive drinking. An alcoholic draws spirits to himself like a magnet. It is not accidental that whisky is referred to as spirits. My observation of hundreds of alcoholics not only indicate that alcohol is the primary cause of possession but that possession is the shackles that perpetuates alcoholism. Once a person becomes an alcoholic and becomes possessed, it is extremely difficult for him to stop drinking. The organization, Alcoholics Anonymous, admonishes its members that they must never take another first drink. Should a reformed alcoholic do so, he may well fall back into his old sorry habits. Also, just because he stopped drinking, does not mean that the entities on board have left. Often they are still there, thirsting for an alcoholic drink. I had the opportunity to examine a group of eighteen AA's for possession; fifteen were possessed.

As remarkable as it may seem, I have relatively little difficulty in helping an alcoholic put aside his drinking habit. The following case histories well illustrate what can be done when the exorcist has an inquiring mind and is persistent.

CASE OF THE ALCOHOLIC

Lena 0. is a superintendent of a manufacturing company. She was irritable at times due to an almost constant domestic problem. Her husband, Henry, was an alcoholic and had been one for some twenty years. When returning home on Fridays, after having spent most of his paycheck at a bar, Henry was abusive and ill-tempered toward his wife. Normally, when not intoxicated, the husband was a gentle and agreeable person.

I was told of the situation by a mutual friend. By using the pendulum, I verified that Henry was spirit possessed by a single intruding personality. There were also nine other spirits around him all eager to find a way to enter his mind. Using the method described in this book, Henry was cleared of these influences and his wife informed of what was done.

A month later Lena reported, "Henry was great for the first three weeks and had stopped drinking. Now he's gone back to drinking. He's about as bad as he always was." Again, using my pendulum, I checked Henry for spirit possession. He was clear. This indicated to me that there had to be an outside influence acting upon him. A list of his drinking buddies was compiled. When they were checked for possession, of the seven listed, only two were spirit possessed. The two were promptly cleared. For the next two months the husband was normal and refrained from excessive drinking. Then he again reverted to his Friday habits and threatening behavior. He was still in trouble.

Something of an unknown nature was bothering the man. Four months passed before the first clue emerged. In a conversation with Lena, she mentioned the bitterness and contempt her son had for his father. The son's attitude was caused by the father's alcoholism. I snatched at this information and immediately checked out the son using my pendulum. Asking questions of the pendulum, which are answered by a yes or no, I discovered nothing unusual about him. He had, however, a number of negative programs. (Negative Programs are explained in Chapter 11.) These were neutralized and a treatment for harmony given for the family. That did it!

As of this writing, more than three years have passed without further excessive drinking by Lena's husband. Not only does a peaceful relationship exist between wife and husband, but what was not anticipated is the close bond which now exists between father and son. The two men are almost inseparable- they cannot do enough for each other.

In this situation, there was another element, other than possession, contributing to the alcoholic problem. This was the negative thought influence the son was directing at his father. The effect of the energy of thought projection upon another can be tremendous. For example, an excellent teacher can vitally influence a child to do well in his studies. The results can be substantial and immediate. What is little understood is how the energy of negative thinking adversely effects the actions of another person. As we shall see later in this book, (See Chap. 11) such negative thoughts do have a devastating effect on those to whom they are directed.

Hundreds of books have been written with harmony, peace of mind and tranquility of spirit as their central theme. Visualization of harmony for others can be exceedingly effective; the results are often spectacular. In Chapter 12, a method is fully explored how one can almost instantly bring about harmony and peace in a turbulent, angry situation.

FANTASY LAND

In the case next described, a clearing was successful for 30-year old Louise V., an alcoholic for 14 years. During that time, her life was filled with romances which turned into nightmares, with close escapes from creditors, and with loss of jobs. Here is her story:

One evening my wife and I visited the home of a family we had but recently met. Our host, John Van Drie, fascinated by the pendulum, wanted to learn more about its use. As a dowser, I know the pendulum can accurately probe the subconscious. Knowledge and facts can be obtained about practically any subject. In the course of our conversation, I spoke about spirit possession. The subject quickened John's interest. He began to ask questions and insisted on exact and detailed answers.

After I had committed myself, with no chance of escape from my position, he asked, "What can you tell me about our daughter, Louise, now living downstairs in the basement?"

I thought, "Why in the world is a girl living in the basement? Why isn't she with us now?" I had put myself on the spot. I had to deliver.

With my pendulum I began to ask questions. In a short while the pendulum told me startling news. Louise was possessed and was more than likely an alcoholic . She had many personality problems . To top it off, her health was poor. How does one tell parents such bleak news face-to-face? As a rule, in such cases, I try to be as diplomatic as I can when reporting negative findings .

This time I could not restrain myself, I exclaimed, "She's a mess, an alcoholic, a real problem! "

"Yes, " agreed the father, with a sigh, "She's all that and more. We simply do not know what to do with her." He then went on to relate what had happened to her during the last twelve months since she had returned home from school .

Louise had been hiding in the basement to escape a hundred imagined fears. She had been anxiously watching television during the Falkland Islands War with the belief that she was destined to marry Prince Andrew. The prince, heir to the throne of England, was a fighter pilot in the war zone. She was fearful that the Prince' s enemies would kidnap her !

"At night, " Her father concluded, "we recently discovered that Louise would steal up to the first floor and raid the liquor cabinet. We had to lock it. We have asked help from the state mental service but have been refused. We are at our wit's end to know what to do. "

After I heard the story of this mixed-up girl, I reflected a moment. I then said with confidence, "Well things are going to change for the young lady, leave it up to me."

The next morning, rested and in the quiet of my room, I cleared Louise of the possessing entities. This took but a few minutes, as I had obtained most of the information about her the previous evening. In Chapter 9 the method used is explained in detail.

Two weeks passed. An excited and incredulous father phoned me. "Louise, " he said, "voluntarily came upstairs the day after you exorcised her. She talked nostalgically about the times the family went to the lake during the summer. It appeared as if she had just awakened from a bad dream. For the first time in a year without prompting she returned to her bedroom upstairs! "

The father continued, "A few days later the neighbors discovered Louise walking about in the snow in house slippers and in her nightgown! She was dazed. She is now in a hospital and we pray she will make a quick recovery."

Louise was apparently unable to orient herself to a way of life that she had almost forgotten. She was as if walking in the shadow of Rip Van Winkle. Louise remained in the hospital for two weeks and then returned home. There was every indication that her mind was once again clear. She began to eat regularly and in about six weeks she had regained her normal weight. In addition, her health rapidly improved. She suffered none of the symptoms of alcohol withdrawal. It wasn't long before she found work as a temporary office worker.

The objective of an exorcism is to normalize the subject's personality and to cancel out all negative influences acting upon the person. The results are not totally predictable, but in general there is a substantial improvement. In Louise's case, there was evidence that something extraordinary had occurred.

My pendulum analysis had indicated Louise had attracted three spirit entities who, to a large extent, were doing her thinking for her. The strongest of these was a mean, negative spirit who under sufficient stress could resort to car robbery, theft, mugging or similar deeds. Since alcoholism was Louise's problem, the spirit probably had the same problem during his/her lifetime on earth. During a drinking session this entity quite likely dominated Louise's mind and compelled her to act irrationally without regard to the consequences to herself or others. In truth, when drinking, she became another person, another personality taking on the unpleasant character of the dominating spirit.

From my experience, when a person has three or more entities influencing his mind and ten to fifty nearby, (Louise had a total of fifteen) it is the pattern of an alcoholic. It is known that even if a person 'goes on the wagon,' stops drinking, the entities usually remain during the person's lifetime.

Similar to my first experience, the clearing of John Van Drie's daughter of spirit possession was the incentive for him to learn and perform the work of an exorcist. Since that time, hundreds of persons have significantly benefited by his dedication to this work.

Not all exorcisms are easy to perform. Some take considerable time and ingenuity. The plight of Glenda related in the next case well illustrates this point.

A CAN OF WORMS

A situation analogous to a can of worms existed in a family of a mixed East Indian-American marriage. Glenda D. was born in India. From her first marriage to an American, she had three sons, ages fifteen to twelve. After her divorce the boys lived with their father. Glenda remarried a Pakistani. Almost every day Glenda would visit the home of her former husband to tend to the needs of her sons. Between members of both families there were bitter recriminations, nasty disputes and arguments. It was an explosive situation.

What further aggravated the problem, the Pakistani was aware of the reality of possession and had learned to project this condition upon another. At this time he was unemployed and in such a state of mind that he was unemployable. When someone would displease him, such as a company personnel director, a neighbor, a welfare worker or even the school principal, they ended up with a few uninvited spirit guests on board. He also was possessed.

Over a period of four months my colleague, John Van Drie, and I labored to identify those persons who were in some way associated with the family and who were possibly possessed. These people lived throughout the world, in the United States and Canada and as far away as India, Australia and England.

As the months went by, with only temporary improvement being reported, we searched for every clue to seek all the basic cause of the family's in-fighting. Of the 804 names submitted to us for analysis, 251 were spirit possessed, a high average of 31 percent. Glenda's numerous long distance phone calls and anxious letters attested to the urgency of her situation.

Finally it was the observation of Glenda's disturbed state of mind that gave us the first clue as to the direction we were to take. We asked ourselves, "Was Glenda unwittingly the catalyst that kept the flame of anger in the family always at the point of eruption?" There was no indication that she was possessed. We decided to include Glenda in a clearing and to emphasize one other point, a special visual projection of harmony for all members of the family.

The results were immediate and exciting. Glenda's final letter written a few weeks after the special visualization was as follows:

"Our life is improving every day. My husband has improved almost 95 percent; the boys also. It is such a welcome change, especially in my oldest son who no longer berates me.

"My husband is laughing and talking, he is no longer silent and disturbed looking. He sleeps better at night and is communicating in a talkative manner.

"I feel we are going to live in peace and not be shrouded in darkness again. Thank you!"

As reported, two years after the clearing, all continues to go well with Glenda and her family. Her husband found employment and there is good will between all members of her large family.

Summarizing the reconciliation, the problem had originally been that of possession with negative thinking and projection of negative thoughts toward each other. The spirit entities were subsequently removed, and this made a decided improvement in relations. Yet negative thinking continued to exist. It resulted in the projection of energy in the form of distrust, vindictiveness and the desire to physically hurt one another. Unconsciously, Glenda, was projecting to the members of her family the expectancy of disharmony, which became the catalyst to bring it about. When her thinking had been altered by the special treatment for harmony, the keystone of cause was removed and disharmony no longer existed.

THE DRUG SCENE

During the past fifteen years, our society has become drug oriented, particularly as reflected in persons under thirty years of age. The effects are the same as with the heavy drinker. These people most often become spirit possessed and experience the same disastrous results as the alcoholic. In severe cases, the victim is completely dominated by the intruding personality.

When drugs in heavy dosages are prescribed by a physician, the patient may become spirit possessed. Certain drugs, like alcohol, cause the body to lose its resistance to intrusion by an entity. Unfortunately, when an earthbound spirit takes residence in a person's mind, in whatever way, the person is in for a bad trip. My associate, John Van Drie, related to me the following account of his work with young drug users.

"Several years ago, a mother requested I check her two sons, Joel thirteen and Brad sixteen, for possession. She had observed, within a short span of time, a marked behavior difference in them. She could not explain it nor could she cope with it. She was divorced and the father had no interest in his sons.

"She related,'Joel, a short time previously, had been an excellent Little League pitcher and a home-run hitter. Now he had dropped baseball completely. Also, Brad wants to quit high school and bum around'.

"My pendulum indicated that the two boys had picked up several negative entities as well as negative programs. They were cleared. The results were almost unbelievable. The younger boy rejoined the Little League, leading his team to the local championship and runner-up in the regionals. The older boy regained his interest in school and found a part time restaurant job .

"The event leading to the possessions was typical. The mother went to a dance and left the youngsters to their own resources. The boys also went out, to a pot party. There, they had smoked marijuana and attracted a host of undesirables to them.

"Six months later the mother asked me to again check her sons as they were becoming unmanageable. As previously, the boys had gone to a pot party and again picked up some uninvited guests. The mother could not understand why the protection placed around her children was not strong enough to keep them free of possession. I explained to her that they had free will and if so inclined could make the same mistakes all over again. It was important to understand the attraction they had to such activity. Peer pressure was irresistibly forcing the boys to participate in a pot party when held.

"I then had to widen my scope of thought. I collected the names and ages of the boy's friends. All were cleared. Also, by visualization, I impressed on their subconscious that such drugs tasted bad, would cause them to become ill and would result in a miserable life for them. This abruptly halted the peer pressure to use drugs. The two boys again returned to more normal activities."

When we recognize the symptoms of a possessed person, we can be helpful in clearing him/her or at least finding someone to give the person aid. The following chapters acquaints the reader with a better understanding of possession and give detailed methods in dealing with it .

PART TWO
Performing the Exorcism

CHAPTER 6

Identifying Spirit Possession

It is first necessary to recognize the possibility that spirit possession exists. Often this is complicated by the medical diagnostician attributing the abnormality to one of a hundred possible causes, each valid in itself. He usually rejects the idea of spirit possession.

With those skilled in the use of the pendulum a probe of the subject's subconscious can be made and secondary personalities, if any, detected. Using the instruction in this book, a person will learn how to remove at a distance the alien personalities from a subject. This will free the subject from all kinds of irrational thoughts and behavior. As a plus to such clearing or exorcism, there is a noticeable improvement in health within a few days, or at most, in a month.

How many people suffer from multiple personality disorders? In the examination of more than 7000 persons, I have found that at least one in twelve is afflicted with this condition. In some segments of our society, the ratio is one in five. Among the criminal element, the ratio is approximately one in every two.

THE PROBLEM PERSONALITY

Before attempting to remove or clear an intruding personality, it is important to be able to identify those persons who may be possessed.

First, what are the effects a subject experiences with a spirit on board?

Frequently, such a person exhibits a lack of energy and weakness in the body. He or she may feel severe depression, disturbed thoughts or irrational thinking. **In general, a possessed person can be identified as one who is extremely negative, severely depressed and who exhibits antisocial behavior.**

The symptoms of possession are similar, if not identical, to schizophrenia. Webster's dictionary defines schizophrenia as "a psychotic disorder characterized by loss of contact with the environment, and by a noticeable deterioration in the level of functioning in everyday life. It is disintegration of personality expressed as a disorder of feeling, thought and conduct."

The people who often complain and express negative feelings and thoughts are prime possession suspects. They have little good to say about the people they meet or about their job and their supervisor. They complain about their lack of money and how rotten the economy is. They are quick to talk about their poor health. Their negativity is like heat to fire; it is always present. The greater the negativity, the more likely the subject is possessed. As can be expected, when the subject is cleared, the negativity diminishes; often it completely disappears.

The severe depression a possessed person falls into has no rational explanation. Moral upliftment or physical help do little to bring them out of their unreasonable behavior.

The antisocial behavior a subject displays is a clear indication that something is wrong. It is normal to try to get along with one's fellow human beings. An overt antisocial act is a strong sign that spirit possession is present. As illustrations of how clear the indications of possession can be, the following cases are presented.

TOMORROW, CINDERELLA

On December 1, 1985 a desperate mother wrote me about the condition of her daughter, age 21.

"Jenny has a severe problem. She behaves like a crazy woman. She lies and cheats and eats everything she sees around the house. She goes from store to store, buys goods and gives them bad checks. She works for a good salary and spends it all on junk food. She refuses to pay her bills. All she does after work is sit and look ugly.

"I love my daughter and want to help her in any way I can, but I don't know where to start. I can't talk to her. Each time I try, she flies at me like a bull ready to charge. If you can help her I would be eternally indebted to you. Please try your best."

The young lady was found to be possessed by a total of 21 unwelcome guests. She was promptly cleared. On February 13, 1986 I received the following letter.

"I apologize for, not writing earlier, but I wanted to have good news to tell you before I responded to the good work you did for us. Jenny is a changed girl! She is not angry like she used to be. She has started paying her bills, and has gone on a diet. Within the last four weeks she lost 20 pounds. She is planning to go as low as 130 pounds. She was 198 pounds.

"I wish to thank you very, very much for the good you have done for us."

As a result of the possession Jenny obviously suffered from a poor self-image, very likely influenced by the most forceful of the possessing spirits controlling her mind. She had a strong fixation of belief that she was unattractive. When the spirit entity left, the irrational appraisal Jenny had of herself ceased to exist.

CASE OF THE NON-STUDENT

The second case was related to me by one of my students. It concerned a 12-year old boy, named Tim. When younger, the child had a long history of illness. Each day when Tim arrived home after school, he would immediately turn on the television set and sit watching it until bedtime. He gave scant attention to his homework and consequently was doing badly in his schoolwork. The child violently resisted any attempt to change his pattern of behavior.

My student checked the boy for spirit entities and found he was possessed. He then cleared the boy.

The father was in for a shock. The next day when he returned home from work, for the first time in years the television set was not turned on. Where was his son? He found the boy in the kitchen quietly doing his homework. A month later the father reported, "My boy is completely changed. He's doing well in school and now has little interest in TV." He added, "If this change hadn't happened right under my nose, I would never believe it could be possible." He concluded, "Thanks, for whatever you did."

Before the exorcism, the boy was analyzed by a psychologist as a potential suicide. Afterwards, the same doctor found no further evidence of suicidal tendencies.

The following true story is another example of an exorcism turning a negative condition into a positive one.

CASE OF THE DISTURBED CHILD

My young stock broker friend listened with interest to my explanation of the work I was doing in clearing persons of spirit possession. He had, after all, become one of the top brokers in his firm, partly as a result of our discussions on how to use the power of the mind.

Shortly after our conversation on possession, he phoned me about a serious problem relating to his daughter. He explained that his 8-year old daughter, Erin, was reported disruptive in class and doing poorly in her school work. Furthermore, she was a discipline problem at home. At night, obviously disturbed, the girl would toss about in her bed.

Anxiously, Tom asked, "Could she be having a problem like you described to me?"

"I'll check this evening." I replied.

That evening I checked Erin using the pendulum and then took the appropriate action. I didn't tell Tom of my findings. A month later a delighted father phoned. "The teachers report my daughter is doing well in her studies and is a pleasure to have in class. Also she sleeps all through the night without disturbance." He added, "I need not tell you she is no longer a problem at home. I'm amazed how changed she it!"

Then I told Tom his daughter had three uninvited boarders who had been directing her antisocial behavior. They had been removed and protection placed around the child. It is unusual for a child of eight to have a spirit possession problem. Perhaps Erin's condition occurred during a surgical operation or severe illness. Children fifteen years or younger generally do not have such problems. Apparently, there is a natural protective barrier a child has that later in life may be partially removed. The loss of protection may be caused by the use of alcohol, drugs or a severe illness. After a clearing, children are usually quick to bounce back to normalcy - probably because they do not have the negative hang-ups often developed with age.

Let us now ask what is happening in cases as just described. What causes spirit possession? Who and what are these spirits? How are they removed? Where do they go when removed? What can be expected when a person is cleared of them?

DETECTING SPIRIT POSSESSION

The following behavior characteristics further identify those persons most likely to be spirit possessed: (1) strong negativity, (2) deep depression, (3) rapid mood change, (4) uncontrolled temper, (5) desire to cause self-inflicted harm, (6) violent behavior, (7) criminal behavior, (8) suicidal tendencies, and (9) a chronic illness. One or two of these characteristics may indicate the possibility of possession.

It is not implied that every person who exhibits any of the above characteristics has a spirit possession problem. Rather, it is an indication that a personality analysis is in order. In particular, a chronic illness may only occasionally be caused by a possession condition.

The strongest candidates for spirit possession are the drug users, alcoholics and criminals. In these groups fifty percent or more are in trouble. Because of the high visibility of such people, the changes effected by an exorcism is often startling.

DUALITY OF PERSONALITY

It is my finding that a multiple personality condition is the same as being spirit possessed. This has been confirmed by others in this field of study. When a person exhibits duality of personality, the extra personality is the spirit of a person who has died. In possession, this spirit has been able to integrate his personality with that of a living person. To further simplify the language in this book, I shall use the terms multiple personality and spirit possession inter-changeably.

At first the presence of a spirit is but slightly noticed by the subject. As the subject gradually loses control of his thoughts and direction, caused by excessive drink, use of drugs or by a severe illness, the invading spirit personality increasingly takes control. At some point, usually early after possession, friends and relatives of the subject start noticing the changes occurring and cannot account for them.

When a strong spirit personality takes charge of a subject, there can be almost complete subjugation of the person's mind. He will act and think as the alien entity dictates. As such an entity usually does not have the best or honorable intentions, the subject soon gets into trouble: first, with his intimate relationships and eventually with the law. If a subject has been so unfortunate as to have attracted an entity with little or no morals, the subject can commit murder, often with but slight provocation.

Physical injury causing unconsciousness can lead to possession. An automobile accident, a severe fall, a battering in a boxing match or football game can permit invasion by a troublesome negative entity.

ARE HOSPITALS SAFE?

In a hospital where many have died, we can expect to find an overabundance of earth-bound spirits. When a patient has been given a general anesthetic for a surgical operation, he may find upon resuming consciousness, that he has one or more extra personalities on board. To forestall possession, a priest is often present when an operation is in progress. Some Catholic priests are aware of this phenomenon; most Protestant ministers are not.

Pain will often drive out a possessing spirit. Many dentists become possessed. It is speculated that the pain induced by the drilling clears the patient, but results in the spirit finding a new home with the dentist! It is perhaps no coincidence that the two professions having the highest suicide rate are the dentists and psychiatrists. The dentist with his drill and the psychiatrist using the electrode for shock treatment, both produce sharp pain. Forceful immoral possessing spirits often urge their host to commit suicide. When I find a -20 or stronger negative entity (See chapter 7, A Measure of Evaluation.) I can say with a fair degree of accuracy that the subject has tried to commit suicide or has contemplated it.

It may be well to turn back the pages of time and examine the general trend of this work which essentially is in the field of parapsychology.

A PARAPSYCHOLOGTST'S OBSERVATIONS

In his book, *After We Die, What Then ?*, George Meek, the distinguished parapsychologist, advances a theory on the possible causes for possession. He speculates on the role the human aura plays in possession.

"Those departing souls who arrive on the lowest of the astral planes find they lack physical bodies and are bewildered by the almost total darkness which seems to surround them. Some may be attracted by the magnetic energy field which emanates from nearby mortals, and which is 'seen' clairvoyantly as light. These mortals may be friends and relatives attending the funeral of the deceased!) Consciously or unconsciously a few of these attach themselves to the magnetic auras of those still in the flesh, thereby finding an avenue of expression by possessing human beings. In such cases, they will influence the possessed person with their own thoughts, impart their own emotions to them, and weaken the will power of the possessed person. In some cases this takeover can be so complete that they will actually control the possessed person's actions, often producing great distress, harmful mental disturbances and suffering.

"So common was the knowledge of spirits and spirit possession during the time of the Apostles that the ability to cast out evil spirits was considered one the most important signs of genuine discipleship. It must be admitted that a considerable portion of the work accredited to Jesus was the casting out of demons." (Meek, p. 70)

THIRTY YEARS AMONG THE DEAD

Another authority on the subject of spirit life is Dr. Carl A. Wickland, M.D. Using his wife as a medium he treated patients in mental hospitals with a success record of 90%. His monumental work, *Thirty Years Among the Dead*, (p.17) speaks eloquently about possession and the tragedy resulting from it.

"These earthbound spirits are the supposed devils' of all ages, devils of human origin, by-products of human selfishness, false teachings and ignorance, thrust blindly into a spirit existence and are held there in a bondage of ignorance. The influence of these discarnated entities is the cause of many of the inexplicable and obscure events of earth life and of a large part of the world's misery. Purity of life and motive, or high intellectuality, do not necessarily offer protection from possession; recognition and knowledge of these problems are the only safeguards."

Dr. Wickland and myself are in agreement in what causes spirit possession. The intrusion of spirits is often due to a natural susceptibility, a devitalized nervous system or unexpected shock. Loss of physical vitality lowers the resistance to invasion, which allows easy access to the encroaching spirits. Most often neither spirit or host realize the other is present.

Dr. Wickland's conclusions of spirit possession is not pretty. Unfortunately, all too often it is an understatement.

"This encroachment alters the characteristics of the sensitive, resulting in a seemingly changed personality. Sometimes this simulates multiple or disassociated personalities, and frequently causes apparent insanity. This may vary in degree from a simple mental aberration to, and including, all types of dementia, hysteria, epilepsy, melancholia, shell shock, kleptomania, idiocy, religious and suicidal mania. This also may including amnesia, psychic invalidism, dipsomania, immorality, functional bestiality, atrocities, and other forms of criminality."

JASTRAM'S VIEWPOINT

Dr. Edward P. Jastram has this to say about interfering personalities who invade the mind of a possessed person. *Body, Mind, and Spirit,* (p. 38) by Dr. Peter Albright.

"Who or what are these entities, and where do they come from? In our culture, persons are not very well educated or prepared for death, as Elizabeth Kubler-Ross has found. The fortunate ones find it to be a pleasant experience, a graduation indeed. Less fortunate people, depending largely on their expectations - You get what you expect - find that death leaves them still functioning as personalities but without an 'earth-suit' to function in. They think they cannot function without one. So they seek entrance to any earth-suit that's handy and still operating which may be open to them. The results of such invasion for the host can be confusing, to say the least. Since the invasion affects primarily the subconscious mind, the host may have little or no awareness of what's going on. If the host is aware of new problems and difficulties, he will normally not be aware of the cause."

ROLE OF THE AURA

The aura around every living person (and earth-bound spirit) is described as being similar to an electro-magnetic field. There are two primary auras, the etheric and the health auras.

The etheric aura has the shape of the body and can be readily photographed by the process known as Kirlian photography. When the hand, for example, is photographed using a color film, a bright bluish glow will be seen outlining the fingers. The movement and extension of this glowing light largely depends upon the thoughts and health of the individual.

You can see the etheric aura. Place your hands on a dark cloth, preferably black velvet. Space the fingers of each hand a half-inch apart from each other. Relax. You will soon see a faint light passing from the fingers of one hand to the fingers on the other hand. The same phenomena can he produced between the fingers of two or more persons.

The health aura is the health barometer of a person. It may extend one or more feet outward from the body. The greater the extension, the greater the vitality of that person. The converse is true. A person with a health aura under six inches is not well; under two inches he may live but a few weeks or months.

With a little training most people can feel the health aura. To do this, you should first vigorously rub the palms of your hands together 10 to 15 times. This will sensitize the palms of your hands. Then place your hands 2 to 4 inches apart, as you would when clapping. Slowly make the motion of clapping but do not touch the hands together. Within a few seconds you should feel a tingling feeling in the finger tips or a magnetic pulling or pushing force on your hands. Some feel warmth. If you have a partner, the same force can be felt by holding one hand up facing the partner's moving hand. This force can be felt at a distance of 125 feet or more.

When the sensitized palm of the hand is slowly moved directly toward a person, the edge of the person's health aura can be felt. Again, the reaction may be a tingling sensation, a feeling of heat or a sensation singular to the experimenter. The aura will appear to be an invisible, irregular balloon extending two to three feet away from the person.

When a disembodied spirit is nearby and is cooperative, a person can readily feel the etheric aura of the spirit. The method is similar to feeling the health aura of a living person.

A few people can see the health aura. It is described as rays emanating from the body. It is multi-colored, the colors corresponding to the emotions and health of the subject. Furthermore, the colors will change with the thoughts of the person.

A discarnated spirit usually has difficulty in seeing a living human body. However, a person's aura can usually be seen, particularly if the spirit has an attachment for earthly things. In possession it is speculated that the spirit enters the aura of the living person. There, the spirit senses the thoughts, motives, feelings, and mental images of the living person. The same phenomena occurs when two people are very close to one another. Their auras intermingle resulting in a telepathic communication between them.

For more information on auras, see the bibliography at the end of this book.

In the next chapter we shall become acquainted with a useful tool in searching for answers whether they concern the living or the dead. The pendulum, coming down to us from antiquity, still is the easiest method to quickly get answers to questions, often impossible by any other means.

CHAPTER 7

Using the Pendulum

Before continuing the diagnosis and treatment for spirit possession, a method must be found quickly to determine the personality of the subject. This is most expeditiously accomplished by using a pendulum. The pendulum is the communication link between a person's subconscious mind and his conscious mind.

When we reach into our subconscious mind we unlock the door to the Superconscious Mind. It is from this Source that all information is available to us. It also provides a convenient access into the subconscious of any subject. (See Figure 1)

BILL COX'S METHOD

Bill Cox in his excellent book, *Techniques of Pendulum Dowsing,* (pp.7-11) has this to say about the pendulum.

"The pendulum has been used for thousands of years as a supersensitive instrument for unlocking the hidden powers of one's subconscious mind and the superconscious mind. A small object made of almost any substance and shape, weighing about an ounce, will serve as a pendulum when attached to a length of thread, string or chain. At the scientific level, the length and vibrational rates of pendulums have for centuries been used to control clock mechanisms, to measure gravity and record the earth's rotation. With pendulum dowsing, we are principally concerned with feelings, mind, energies, motion and gravity.

"Historically, dowsing, *virgula divina* or divining with the rod shape in Europe, can be traced back to the 15th century. Cave wall paintings indicate primitive man indulged in some form of divining in prehistoric times. The early Egyptians and Polynesians worked with the pendulum. The Chinese use of the pendulum can be traced back to 4,000 B.C. Evidence of divining with the pendulum appears in the historical records of ancient Greece. By the 4th Century A.D., the art of dowsing with the divining rod found its way to Cyprus.

"Recent estimates suggest there are at least 200,000 professionally active or amateur dowsers in the world today. In addition, thousands of humans now living, have tried dowsing one or more times. Uncounted millions have witnessed, heard or read about it. Many of the world's finest producing water and oil wells, and mines have been pin-pointed by dowsers. Difficult missing person searches have also been successfully conducted with the help of skilled dowsers."

Many dowsers hold to the theory that all materials of every kind radiate energy which is sensed by the dowser. To me, the energy theory is unacceptable. Information can be derived, using a dowsing tool, from a location half way around the world with the same ease as in a neighbor's lot. Cox offers an explanation which more closely coincides with my experience.

"While employing the psychic faculty, the dowser (locater) With the aid of a physical instrument - and a previously determined dowsing code - poses a question to his/her subconscious mind. The objective is to gather certain information, usually at a distance, regarding a person, creature, form, substance, time or place. The answer thus obtained comes from the intuition, beyond the limitations of one's actual logical and reasoning processes. One's intellect initiates the activity and eventually summarizes the findings.

"The secret to successful dowsing lies in one's ability to hold a clearly stated, mentally posed question in mind. The clarity of the query is essential. Hazy questions bring on confused answers. The inquiring mind should frequently restate the question, preferably one inquiry at a time. Multiple questions with unskilled pendulists frequently produce conflicting information.

"Those who say that dowsing is a gift only bestowed on them and a precious few, are strictly on an ego trip. This belief is an outright fallacy. True, some people learn and adapt quickly. Most dowsers who withstand the tests of time and accuracy, generally admit that dowsing finesse is usually acquired through the tribulations of trial and error and continued practice.

"Factors which hamper the dowsing effort include: lack of concentration; needless superstitions; a poorly defined dowsing code, and imperfect coordination between one's mind and the hand-held instrument."

Researcher Christopher Bird speaks of the pioneer dowsing work in unorthodox medicine by the French priest, Father Jean Jurion. *(The Divining Hand)* p. 291.

"Jurion's battle with medical authority in following Christ's admonition to 'heal the sick' has encouraged many lay persons among his compatriots to do likewise. Today, over one hundred medical dowsers, officially recognized as a professional group by the Ministry of Labor, practice their art in France."

In this country the pendulum is being used increasingly in health matters. The Cameron Aurameter pendulum was specifically designed to find openings in a person's aura, which may indicate locations of disease. As a useful tool, John Van Drie employs the pendulum to detect and define allergies, to determine the proper dosage of vitamins, and as a guide to proper diet. For each of her patients Dr. Sybil Fitch of Naperville, Illinois, examines over 400 foods and substances using the pendulum. Dr. C.W.M. Wilson, M.D., in Scotland makes extensive use of the pendulum in diagnosing allergies. Dr. Lauri Campbell of Detroit, Michigan, uses the pendulum to verify his medical diagnosis.

PARAMETRIC ANALYSIS CHART

As a useful device I use the pendulum to obtain the answers to questions on personality, usually of persons I have never met and who are at a distance from me. My code is a clockwise circle to indicate a 'Yes' answer, and a counterclockwise circle to indicate a 'No' answer. Frequently, the size of the circle will have meaning for me.

In William Finch's pioneer work, *Pendulum and Possession*, the *Parametric Analysis Chart* (Figure 2) was developed to obtain detailed answers about a client. The lower portion of the chart has a 180 degree sector divided from 0 to 100. If a specific question can be answered by a number, the pendulum will swing to that number. The chart may be used to determine a percentage. For example, using the pendulum in this way, I can usually quite accurately pinpoint the percentage of health a person has at that moment. (100 percent, being the best health the person has ever attained, usually at birth.) The upper portion of the chart is divided into -30 to +30. This portion is used when making a personality analysis or to determine the type of possessing entity.

For accurate pendulum readings, I must be rested and emotionally undisturbed. After about two hours work and 150 pendulum readings, fatigue sets in. It then becomes more difficult for me to get accurate readings. Since 1983, my average work load has been the diagnosis of fifty persons per week involving about five pendulum readings for each person. My accuracy is from 85 to 95 percent for those questions I ask repeatedly. It was the noted pianist, Artur Rubinstein who said, "When I fail to practice one day, I can notice the difference. When I fail to practice two days, my audience notices the difference!" If you want to be an expert in using the pendulum: practice, practice, practice!

READING THE PENDULUM

The pendulum I use has a 1/2 inch round lead as a weight which is suspended on a 6-inch long beaded chain. Attached to the other end of the chain is a 3/8 round necklace bead which serves as the knob. The pendulum may be held by either hand whichever feels most comfortable. Usually the elbow is supported on the desk or arm of the chair.

When inquiring whether or not a person is spirit possessed, first position the pendulum over the center of the *Parametric Chart*. Relax. Allow the pendulum to rotate in a clockwise direction. This is called the seeking position.

Ask: "Is this person possessed and if so, how many spirit entities are influencing him/her in any way?"

If the pendulum swings from left to right, the answer is none. If yes, the pendulum will count the total entities, both negative and positive, by swinging to a number on the lower position of the chart from 0 to 100.

In determining the characteristics of the possessing entities within the mind of the subject, you must first firmly fix in your mind the definition of each positive or negative number. Refer to *A Measure of Evaluation*, page 105, for the definitions.

Allow your pendulum to rotate in the seeking position and then ask for the negative number closely identifying the strongest negative entity. The pendulum will swing to that number. Continue to ask for the next strongest one until all are identified. When the count has been completed, the pendulum will swing straight up and down, referred to as the neutral position. Record the data.

Should you desire to count numbers greater than 100, you may count out loud allowing your pendulum to rotate in a clockwise direction. When the pendulum slows down, you are nearing the number sought and when it stops, you have the number.

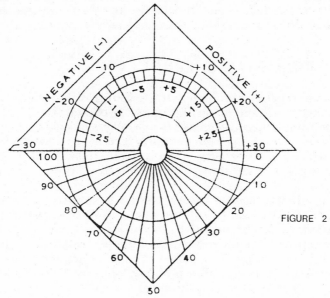

FIGURE 2

PARAMETRIC ANALYSIS CHART

Chart courtesy of *Pendulum and Possession,* by William J. Finch.

AMERICAN SOCIETY OF DOWSING

The *American Society of Dowsing* headquartered in Danville, Vermont, has done much to publicize and train people how to use the pendulum and other devices to find answers to almost every conceivable question. The society has thousands of members throughout the United States. Further reading on how to use the pendulum is suggested in the bibliography section.

THE ANALYSIS

When there are indications that a person has a multiple personality problem, I use the pendulum to ask questions about the person. I ask, "Is this person possessed?" If the answer is yes, I ask, "What are the total number of spirit entities around this person and within his mind?" The pendulum will swing to the lower section of the Parametric Chart, 0 to 100. There may be up to 75. I record the number. This total will include all negative and positive entities within the subject's mind as well as all those in the vicinity who have been attracted to him/her. The vicinity entity has little, if any, effect upon the subject.

Then I ask, "Give me an indication of the strongest spirit personality within the person's mind." The pendulum will swing to a number on the upper left quadrant of the chart, identifying the character of the strongest negative entity. I then ask for the next strongest and continue until all the negative spirit intruders are identified. Usually there are an average of three controlling entities. As the positive entities normally are not a problem to the subject, I do not measure them.

In every case the spirits referred to are earthbound spirits who are on this earth plane. Their reasons for being here are varied. Some know of no other place to live so choose a suitable comfortable location here to inhabit. Others, are attracted to friends and relatives and follow them around. The type who cause a great deal of trouble to the living are classified as negative entities. These are antisocial and desire to experience riotous living again. They are most likely to possess a person. Among these are the disembodied spirits who desire to get intoxicated with liquor or drugs. They may have been former criminals and are looking for a host body to continue their career of crime. In every instance they bring to the possessed person untold misery, physical and mental.

Again using the lower chart, scaled 0 to 10, I ask, "How many entities are in the person's home?" There may be negative thoughts directed at the person. I ask,"How many negative energies are influencing this person?" Also, I ask, "How many negative programs has this person accumulated in his/her lifetime?" Using the lower chart, scaled 0 to 100 for percentage, I continue to ask, "What is this person's state of health?" Finally, I ask of the person's Higher Self, "Do I have permission to clear this person?" When possible, I get the names of family members and close associates and check them also.

In this work it is important to keep records to understand what is happening to your client over a period of months or even years. I use the form, Request for Healing and or Clearing shown in the back of this book. See Figure 3. This also becomes my report to the client. For a better understanding what has been done, I send additional information. See Figures 3 and 4 in the back of this book.

Often a person unknown to me, will have a strong negative influence over the person being evaluated. The unknown person must be identified and his/her negative influence neutralized. This must be done before the person, recently exorcised, is able to recover completely. Usually, a person very close to the victim, quite unknowingly, is the culprit. Such was the case of Lena's husband, described as the alcoholic. Although he was no longer possessed, he kept on drinking. The case was solved when it was discovered the man's son was projecting, quite unknowingly, negative thought energy toward him. This caused the father's distress and resulted in his continued drinking. What may have started out to be a simple request for a clearing of an individual, all too often ends up with a dozen or so persons being analyzed. Of this group, some also may have to be cleared.

When making a personality analysis, more accurate readings can be obtained when the pendulist knows little about the client. The pendulist must constantly guard himself from letting his reasoning conscious mind influence his subconscious. Should the conscious mind decide it is ridiculous for a particular person to be possessed, the subconscious will oblige. The person will be given a clear bill of health even though the truth may be otherwise. For this reason, I initially request that only the full name, age and town be given to me. In this way, I am not unduly influenced by the opinions and observations of others. For proper feedback and continued treatment, the name and address of the person making the request should be given. Since the analytical process may take 30 to 45 minutes, spurious information or names of persons not remotely involved with the victim should not be submitted for analysis.

As a matter of interest, it is not absolutely necessary to know the name of the client. Should the requester but think of the person needing help, the exorcist using the pendulum can obtain all the information necessary to perform an exorcism. Of course, without a name no record can be kept nor follow-up made.

OUR LIMITATIONS

A word of caution is appropriate here. As an exorcist, one must be aware that our emotions can distort or bias the information coming to us from the pendulum or from our intuition. Should we try to analyze a person close to us, often we are inaccurate. Our conscious or critical mind will distort facts colored by our personal feelings. Our conclusions, then, are often based upon our emotions and not on facts. Should we try to analyze our son-in-law, for example, who is at odds with our daughter, our feelings may well distort our findings. Such diagnosis is suspect.

HEALING BLOCKS

There is a sequel to the case of Louise V. described in Chapter 5. As the reader will recall, Louise, who had been an alcoholic, was cleared of entities and within a comparable short period of time returned to the mainstream of normal life.

After six months, I gave no further thought to the follow-up of Louise's condition. Her father was a competent exorcist by this time and I therefore placed her in his hands. A curious thing happened. Her father was not able to keep his daughter clear of other entities that she again attracted. When he threw out one group of entities, others would quickly take their place.

Two years later, quite by accident, I learned Louise was in a mental hospital in very poor health and rapidly failing. Her condition was diagnosed as schizophrenia. She also was suffering from a crippling arthritis condition. My pendulum indicated that she was again very badly possessed. The pendulum also verified her poor state of health. She was promptly cleared.

Within a few days Louise responded to the exorcism. She phoned her sister to whom she had not spoken for over a year. She was lucid and gave every sign of normalcy. Within a few weeks her health showed remarkable improvement. In eight weeks her weight increased from 85 to 105 pounds. The arthritic condition responded favorably to treatment. She was able to return home for a visit to the tearful delight of her parents.

Why wasn't Louise's father, an accomplished exorcist, not able to protect his daughter from disruptive entities? Why was the healing ineffective that he gave her? This condition often occurs between a healer and his relatives and close friends. The healer finds he is completely powerless to help them.

The healer's conscious mind interferes with the process of exorcism or healing. It sends out signals of doubt to the subconscious mind. It goes somewhat like this: "Yes, I can heal that person 5000 miles away or that stranger who seeks my aid. I have done it many times. But I know that my dearest friend is very, ill, I see him suffering, I feel his pain. Can I really help him?" The condition observed is not a subconscious one; it becomes a conscious real situation. It remains in the healer's conscious mind where healing cannot occur. Even Harry Edwards, England's foremost spiritual healer, was unable to arrest the failing health of his dear friend, Jack Webber. I, too have this same problem. There is a obvious and simple solution.

When a healer has an emotional connection to a person, the healer should not attempt to diagnose or heal that person. The healer's conscious mind interferes with the healing. The healer should find another healer, one who has no emotional attachment to the person needing help. The alternate healer may well be successful in the healing or exorcism

A MEASURE OF EVALUATION

Bill Finch in his excellent thesis on spirit possession, *The Pendulum and Possession,* created a yardstick to identify and classify a personality. The personality may be a living person or a spirit entity. The entity may be a possessing spirit. When the exorcist makes a positive identification of the type and strength of the invading spirits, he can be more effective by varying his approach to the exorcism.

With modification of the original definitions given by Finch, on a scale of -30 to +30, using a pendulum, a living person or a spirit entity is analyzed as follows: (Refer to Chart 2. *Parametric Analysis*)

0 Neutral or balanced mind. This is the most sought condition. It is in the majority.

-5 Has little concern for others or truthfulness. Such a person would make an outstanding used car salesman or politician.

-10 Indicates a basically dishonest tendency, falling between misdemeanor and felony. This person may typically be a shoplifter or petty thief.

-15 Characterized by being involved in car thefts, robberies or similar deeds. May beat his wife and children.

-20 A dangerous criminal. Will commit murder with provocation or when under duress.

-25 Highly dangerous. Will kill with slightest provocation and for little reason.

-30 A mass murderer. Will kill for the love of killing. Needs no reason to kill, nor will anything of a moral nature dissuade the person from killing.

(Fortunately for society, - and for the exorcist - there are not many such spirit entities around. Of some 8000 persons analyzed, I have found but 8 with a -30 reading.)

On the other hand, the positive spirit group may have some beneficial effects on the individual. As a rule they do not cause as much trouble as the negative group. Those rated +20, and greater, are troublesome and when removed, the subject is in a better state of mind.

+5 The person has broad thinking and stability; May be a highly qualified teacher or counselor.

+10 A person of great wisdom and sound metaphysical thinking. This person has the attributes of a mystic.

+15 A person firm in ideals and ideas, the typical evangelist.

+20 An intolerant person, inflexible in his/her ideas. Look for a minister determined to reform the congregation.

+25 A person who is stubborn in thought, unrelenting, and unforgiving. "The Hanging Judge."

+30 This is the crusader whose belief is "Kill, it is God's will!"

The above readings are not to be interpreted to mean that a person measuring -15, for instance, will beat his wife or commit a crime. It simply means that under sufficient stress the individual could behave in this way.

It is not absolutely necessary to learn everything about a possessing spirit. The above ratings, determined by a pendulum, are usually sufficient.

It will sometimes occur that a strong positive entity will team up with an equally strong negative entity, each not knowing the other is present. The subject is exposed to the worst of both worlds. He may commit brutal crimes and feel they were justified. He may feel no remorse or pangs of conscience. Typically, a criminal who feels justified in murdering prostitutes may have this combination. When I make a personality analysis, I check only for negative entities, as even the least negative ones are troublesome. Nevertheless, all other entities present, positive or negative, are counted as a group and cleared as a group.

PROBING THE SUBCONSCIOUS

When using the pendulum, usually a simple answer to the question, "Is this person possessed?" is sufficient information required for an exorcism. If, after a clearing, the subject does not show a positive response, then it becomes necessary to find the cause of the negative attitude and actions. There are a number of questions the inquirer may ask to get at the root of cause. Using a pendulum and appropriate charts, the following line of inquiry is suggested.

1. "Is this person possessed?" If the answer is yes, I ask, "May I have an indication of the strongest negative entity?" Use the scale of 0 to -30 to identify the character of the entities. Then ask, "What is the second strongest?" Continue to ask until all the entities have been identified.

2. "What is the total number of entities within the mind of this person and those nearby, both negative and positive?"

3. "Is there a part of this person inviting entities on board?" When a yes answer is indicated, other questions may have to be formulated.

4. "May I have an indication of the self-image of the conscious personality?" The lower percentage scale on the Parametric Chart can be used.

5. "May I have an indication of the self-image of the

subconscious personality?" Again, the percentage scale may be used. A comparison of the self-image of the conscious mind and subconscious mind will indicate a conflict if one exists.

6. "What is the intelligence level of this person? What percentage of that intelligence is the person using?" Use the percentage scale.

7. "What are the total psychological problems this person has related to mother, father, children, mate, peers, duty, religion, fear, disharmony, falsehood, negative self-programs, negative thoughts of others, desire for companionship, hate, envy, or spirit entities?"

To discover the psychological problems, use the 0 to -30 scale on the Parametric Chart. Allow the pendulum to swing to the total score for these items. As each item is called out, the pendulum will swing toward the neutral, subtracting from the total if that item is part of the psychological trouble.

8. "What are the worldly problems this person is experiencing related to his job, the environment, money, or people?"

The scale of 0 to +30 is used to measure a problem related to the physical world we live in. The pendulum will indicate a total score for all such problems. As the worldly problems are called off, the pendulum will move toward zero or neutral indicating the extent of each problem.

9. "What is this person's wholeness percentage? How many incongruent parts of this person are there which are acting in opposition to the wholeness of this person?"

The lower scale may again be used, first as a percentage, 0 to 100, and then for a quantity, 0 to 10.

10. "Based on the best health attained since birth as 100 percent, what is this person's present health percentage?"

11. "Is there some part of the personality inducing illness to fulfill some need quite unknown to the conscious self?" When the answer is yes other questions must be formulated and asked.

12 . "May I have an indication of the negative influences acting upon this person?" Usually there are but few such influences. The lower scale may be used for 0 to 10.

13 . "May I have an indication of the negative programs involving deprivation, anger and fear?" Use the lower scale for 0 to 100.

14. "Is it appropriate to attempt to improve this situation?"

15 . "Do I have permission from this person's Higher Self to give help? "

The answers to the above line of inquiry will have increasingly more meaning as the pendulist gains experience in this work. When the same question is asked and answered many times, the pendulist will become better guided in the direction to take.

NEGATIVE PROGRAMMING

Most of us are to some extent negatively programmed. During our lifetime, particularly in our formative years, we have often been given information or instruction which is false. This misinformation is buried deep in our subconscious with little awareness that it exists. In our adult years these false ideas often interfere with our health, personal relationships, our work, and our social and political viewpoint.

For those who have developed the skill of probing the subconscious by using the mind alone without using the pendulum, it is possible to go directly to the subconscious of a person to determine the negative programming. The following two cases illustrate this procedure.

The first case is of a woman living in Florida, whom I knew only through correspondence from her friend. She had a continuous headache and the medical profession could find no physical cause. Using the simple method suggested by Arthur Ford, I relax and then hear answers from the subconscious of the person I wish to contact. This is called clairaudience. Using this method I obtained the following information:

Rev. M. "I wish to speak to the subconscious of Irene S. Tell me the basic cause of the headaches you are experiencing."

Irene. "I need to go back many years to a time when I was very little. My mother told me when I was naughty I would become ill to pay for my bad behavior. Now, I have done a lot of mischief to a woman I hate. This has brought on the headaches."

Rev. M. "You have a simple solution. You must forgive her as well as forgive yourself."

Irene. "How do I do that?"

Rev. M. "Assuming the name of the woman is Gloria, this is how you can do it. Say and believe this: Gloria, I forgive you and let you go to your good. All is finished between us now and forever. Gloria, you forgive me and let me go to my good. All is finished between us now and forever." (From a Unity treatment for harmony.)

At the end of the conversation, I picturized her outflowing love to all around her and drawing love to herself. I saw her in excellent health, radiant and feeling well. The last incomplete report indicated that she was feeling better. This woman had no conscious awareness that she had been programed as a child to expect punishment for her misdeeds.

FRUSTRATION

The second case is of a man about 50 years old who was off and on the bottle. He was off after I cleared him, and on again a few weeks later. As I was making little progress, the direct approach to the subconscious suggested itself.

Rev. M.: "I wish to speak to the subconscious of Joe 0. Can you tell me what is troubling you? Perhaps I can help you."
Joe: No one can help me. I'm too far gone. I'm stuck in a rut. I hate my work. Everyday is a chore. Every weekend I want to blow it all away. I want to cry."
Rev. M.: "Perhaps you should cry, release all that frustration within you."
Joe: "I look at my life and see no end of misery. I don't know where I'm going. I see no end."

At this point I explained to Joe what happened to me in a similar circumstance and how I solved the problem. Whether this discussion had a direct effect on Joe's life, I have no way of knowing. I again checked him for possession and cleared him. From the last report, he is drinking less and behaving much better to his wife even when drinking.

HEALTH

A poor state of health of an individual is often an indication of possession. Using the pendulum, the condition of a person's health can be indicated as a percentage of the best health the person has ever had. Usually the best health, or 100 percent, was at birth or shortly afterwards.

When a person is possessed, the percentage of health is rarely above 50 percent. After a clearing, the percentage will usually improve 10 to 30 percent within a comparatively short time. During a follow-up, the health percentage is another yardstick to ascertain if new entities have come aboard. The percentage health, therefore, is another clue to what is happening.

The following chart is based on an average age of 40. It should be pointed out that a child, 10 years old, would not be in good health at 60 percent. On the other hand, a person of 70 years or more may be considered in very good health if measured at that percentage.

PERCENTAGE	HEALTH
100% to 90%	Excellent
85% to 70%	Very Good
65% to 55%	Good
50% to 40%	Fair
35% to 25%	Poor
20% and below	Very Poor

WHOLENESS

The state of mind is an important indicator whether or not a person is suffering interference by possessing entities. The relationship in a person's mind between the three parts of the personality, the conscious, subconscious, and Superconscious, determines the degree of enlightenment the person has attained. This relationship has been labeled wholeness, a term coined by Dr. Edward Jastram, essentially meaning enlightenment.

Jastram, a leading advocate of distance exorcism; simplifies his explanation by using Huna terms to describe the three parts of man . He refers to the conscious mind as the Middle Self, the subconscious mind as the Low Self, and the Superconscious Mind as the High Self. Refer to Figure 1. In a talk given to the American Society of Dowsers at Danville, Vermont on Sept. 1984, he spoke of wholeness as a measure of the effectiveness of an exorcism. He explained as follows:

"I ask for the wholeness percentage of the individual. I like to know where he is . You ask what percentage wholeness means. It is the unimpeded, clear and instant communication, back and forth, between the three parts of the personality. It is a measure of how completely a person uses his attributes, his personality and his potential. Of course, nobody is one hundred percent.

"In the case of a person who has entities aboard, the entities are almost a complete block to access to the High Self. My experience indicates that when I measure the percentage wholeness of such a person, using the pendulum, I almost always get considerably less than one percent . In fact, I get ridiculous measurements such as .00002 percent. There is simply no communication with the High Self in a case like that

"A lot of my work has to do with people I never met, and probably never will . Often I don't get feedback . What I like to know is how effective I am in the work I am doing. I concocted this measurement of wholeness with its definition. If I get rid of a bunch of entities and other negative effects, then a person's wholeness should go up, and it does . Let me give an example .

"This is a case of a young man of eighteen. At the age of about sixteen he disassociated himself from reality; he became catatonic. He would communicate with no one. Through treatment, he improved, but while beginning to communicate, he would do nothing. He had no will, no volition. He lived in his parents' home in complete idleness. His father came to the conclusion that his son had entities on board and therefore contacted me. It seemed to be an emergency so that night I concentrated on the removal of the entities. At that point he measured about .0002 percent wholeness! There was a complete blockage between his low self and High Self.

"The day after the clearing, he was up to 5 percent. Percentage-wise this was enormous. The second day he was up to 10 percent and each succeeding day he improved further. Plotting a curve of his advancement coincided with a typical growth curve, giving validity to the readings. The percentage of growth increases rapidly at first and then tapers off as you approach maturity. I felt this person was approaching maturity at too low a value on the curve. When he leveled out at 20 percent, I did a careful job of removing a whole bunch of negative programs. His growth started all over again. This was another confirmation of the feeling I had done something. Later I was to learn my pendulum readings had mirrored the actual progress of the boy.

"Please understand that all of this was taking place at the subconscious level and may not yet have been visible at the conscious level. There were some physical signs of improvement. He had reached 40 percent, which is extraordinarily high. There is every possibility this boy will become a marvelous and productive individual."

Jastram's use of the pendulum is but one of the dowsing techniques to obtain information from the subconscious. Other dowsers may specialize in the L-rod, Y-fork or a number of other more exotic instruments. The natural or trained psychic can obtain the same information without an instrument. Whatever method is used, each ultimately taps the Superconscious where all information is known.

When a practitioner of exorcism becomes skilled in using a method to probe the subconscious of his client, the information to accomplish his task becomes available. With this information he can tailor his method to suit the situation.

When one becomes familiar with the symptoms of possession, which are often highly visible, the possessed person can be identified and helped. In distant exorcism, I use a pendulum to verify my subconscious impressions. The next chapter describes how the pendulum is used to detect possessing intruders.

CHAPTER 8

Exorcism at a Distance

Webster defines an exorcism, 'as the act of casting out or expelling evil spirits. By challenges, prayers, or ceremonies it is a deliverance from unclean spirits.' I define an unclean spirit as one who is negative and evil in character and one who causes trouble to the host body.

WIPING THE SLATE CLEAN

It is my observation that much of the abnormal social behavior of people we meet is caused by spirit possession. When such people are cleared of possessing spirits, there is an astonishing and welcome change for the better. Often the subject of the exorcism does not realize at first that his thinking and attitude has changed. His immediate family and associates are usually the first to notice a change in him. He simply feels he is normal and does not recall that he has been other than in his present state of mind. Somewhat later, perhaps in a week, he may notice his likes and dislikes have altered. Should he have been a hard drinker, whiskey no longer tastes good and he refuses it when offered. The criminal suddenly ceases his immoral activities. The estranged son, returns home to the welcoming arms of his parents.

When cleared, the chronically ill person shows a rapid increase in health. The scheduled surgical operation is canceled and the attending physician is amazed at the effectiveness of his treatment. The physician usually attributes the recovery to an unexpected remission.

Formerly a negative person, the cleared person begins to realize that he lives in an attractive world. The people around him are getting friendlier. If married, he cannot understand why he had been nasty to his wife. He goes out of his way to make up for the misery he caused her. His mood turns to optimism. He starts being what he was before the possession, perhaps turning back the calendar some twenty years! The result of an exorcism is a joyous occasion to witness.

NOT HER PROBLEM!

The following case illustrates what can happen after a distant exorcism is performed. It is presented in chronological sequence. The subject's name has been changed to insure privacy. On January 18, 1985 I received the following letter from Clara G.

'I saw you on Damien Simpson's T.V. program. You mentioned you could help people. I wonder if you would help Mary M., age 42. She has been seeking help to no avail.'

On January 30, 1985, I answered Clara's letter.

'Mary was possessed. She has been cleared. There should be a noticeable change for the better, both in disposition and in health. People who are possessed whether obviously or not, have a rough time with personality and health. Nothing seems to work for them.

'Enclosed is material which will explain the process of an exorcism as well as the power of the mind.'

On February 11, 1985, I received a note from the subject, Mary M.

'My name is Mary M. Clare G. wrote you in my behalf regarding my health, emotional decline and an obsession for alcohol consumption. This was more than two months ago and I wish to tell you that in addition to regaining my health, I have a complete change in attitude, returning to the personality I had before this affliction. I also experienced a spiritual awakening during this time.

'May I say I am a happy, functioning person once again. I rejoice in this as do my loved ones.

'Thank you so very much for your healing intercession on my behalf.'

Note the discrepancy in time in which Mary M. recalled her past afflictions, two months. The actual time the sequence of events took place was less than a month, between January 18 and February 11. There were actually only 12 days between the exorcism and Mary M.'s letter. This is typical of an exorcism. The subject often has difficulty in recalling problems and will relate them to the distant past. In reality the problems belong to the departed entity and not to the subject.

My pendulum findings indicated Mary M. was an alcoholic. It was not appropriate to relate that detail to Clara G.

THE SCIENTIST

A like process of depossession is explained by Christopher Bird in his book, *The Divining Hand.* Bird describes the work of his friend and colleague, Dr. Edward P. Jastram, in clearing people of spirit possession.

Since his retirement from Texas Instruments as Chief of Research, Dr. Jastram has given his attention to research of spirit possession of persons by nonmaterial entities that cause both physical and mental abnormalities. Jastram has demonstrated that by using a pendulum, a thorough analysis of any individual's personality may be swiftly and accurately made by communicating with the person's subconscious mind. He has found that the injury of a foreign presence may range from slight to a complete takeover of a person's body and mind.

As a typical case, Jastram cites the following sequence of events: (Bird, p. 298)

'A middle-aged woman had been praised for her reliability and industry as a domestic worker for a group of households on a Caribbean Island. Suddenly she became surly and evasive, addicted to drink, and embroiled in fights and lost weekends, during one of which she broke her leg in a fall from her bicycle. All of her employers and friends were horrified by the dramatic change that had come over her.'

When the situation was brought to Jastram's attention, his pendular analysis indicated the presence of three personalities on board, which were very negative in character. Steps were taken to eliminate them and a recheck of her personality indicated that they were gone. Within a week, her personality had returned to normal. During Jastram's handling of this case there was no personal contact between the patient and himself. The whole situation was worked on in absentia.

Jastram had long recognized that spirit possession affected the subject by producing fear, depression, poor judgment and ineffectual decisions. In addition, there was a loss of problem solving ability, a feeling of inferiority and a deterioration of the capacity for creativity. Frequently, possession was accompanied by physical disabilities such as allergies, loss or gain in weight and serious internal illnesses.

Jastram cited another case which involved a young widow who struggled to rear two children on her own. After the children had grown and left home, she directed her energies to church work where she was recognized as a conscientious and productive worker. Suddenly her fellow workers became aware of a marked change in her personality revealed by her tendency to make nasty remarks. Soon her language became so coarse that the women about her began avoiding her company. When the situation reached Jastram's ears, he found that the woman was being controlled by a strong negative entity which he promptly removed.

The next day the woman telephoned all her friends and in tears apologized for her nasty behavior. She returned to her normal cheerful self and has remained so ever since. Jastram reported, 'Her recovery was one of the quickest I have ever known. She knew nothing of the work I had performed but after her return to normal, said she had awakened from a bad dream.'

Asked how, once having detected alien personalities with his pendulum, he is able to remove them, Jastram explained that he gets into a state of mind in which his brain emits alpha waves (See footnote) enabling him to identify the dowsed alien personalities to be exorcised. He then tells them who they are, where they are and what they are to do. During this process, he usually take three or four deep breaths to accumulate energy. He the then sends the energy (Mana) to what has been called by the Hawaiian Kahunas, or shaman priests, his Higher Self. At this point he usually get an intuitive indication of what is occurring in the person he is seeking to help. He takes the positive approach that the job has been satisfactorily completed and has effective results. He equates the whole process to a highly efficient prayer mechanism.

Dr. Jastram sums up his experience. 'The question had been raised as to the prevalence of the entity invasion problem. The answer from William J. Finch, who had worked in this area for many years, is that twenty-five percent of the population have this problem. My own experience would indicate that the proportion is at least that high. Many of the physical and mental difficulties coming to the attention of the medical profession, particularly the chronic ones, may be related to this phenomenon.'

(Footnote) By controlled relaxation the brain wave frequency can be reduced to the alpha range of 15 down to 7 cycles per second. This is the state of mind where a person has direct access to the subconscious. This brain vibration range, however, is completely disassociated from the high vibration signifying a person's spiritual evolution. (Refer to Chapter 4, item 10, *WE DON'T DIE)*

THE COMPASSIONATE EXORCIST

Walter H. Woods, in his talk at the 1985 Sixth West Coast Dowsers' Convention, has this to say about spirit possession:

'The vicinity entities are not a problem; the ones that react with a person are. I object to a type of exorcism where one merely drives a spirit out of a building or out of a person. What is the spirit going to do? He will either try hard to get back into the same person or find somebody else to possess. That is not desirable.

'What I do is ask my spirit guides to take care of the situation. When I make the request, they have channels already set up to do the work. There are skilled personnel available who immediately pick up the spirit person and take off. This happens fast. The guides either hospitalizes (See footnote) them or join them with their friends. Whatever is appropriate in their world is done. I do not get further involved. This process insures that the spirits do not come back. It also relieves the exorcist of a hard time for interfering with them. This is an effective method to deal with possessing spirits.'

(Footnote) A patient in great pain is often sedated with drugs. When such a person passes over, there is often no consciousness that a transition has occurred between the living and spirit worlds. The person then carries over to his new environment the consciousness of being ill and in pain. Such a spirit person is hospitalized in that other world in hospitals similar to those we have here. The Tibetans well understand this characteristic of dying. They do not administer pain killing drugs to a dying person. They keep the person conscious to his very last breath.

EVALUATION OF SPIRIT ENTITIES

It is important to know the nature and kind of spirit personalities who exist within the mind of a subject. With an evaluation of the invading entities, their personality characteristics can be detailed fairly accurately. The subject will also exhibit a similar personality profile. When a close dead relative is identified as being the possessing spirit, there is a striking personality resemblance. When a strong negative entity is present, the subject can be suicidal. Such an entity will urge the victim to commit suicide, or worse, to commit a murder. These persons should be cleared without delay.

When the entity measures on the extreme negative level, take special precautions! Such entities are dangerous and the exorcist must be firm and operate through an intermediary. If you're foolish enough to drive your car 150 miles per hour, at least check your brakes and fasten your seat belt! Figuratively, I did neither when I tackled my first multiple mass murderer. Let me tell you about a lesson that I learned the hard way.

THE FREEWAY KILLER

When I first started this work, I made the mistake of speaking directly to the possessing spirits. I was not aware how evil some of them could be. One almost killed me! Since that time, I let my obliging spirit guide, George, on the other side do the work. This is what happened.

The newspapers reported the capture in California of the 'Freeway Killer.' His name was Bonen, who allegedly had murdered 41 boys and young men. He dumped the bodies of his victims on the freeways.

'An interesting situation,' I thought, 'Let's take a look at this man and see what makes him tick.'

My pendulum revealed that he was possessed by the strongest negative spirit that I had yet encountered since beginning this work. It was -30. This level is defined on the Parametric Chart as a mass murderer who kills for enjoyment. (See Chapter 7, *A MEASURE OF EVALUATION*)

'No trouble, 'I concluded, 'I'll take care of you in a hurry.' I performed an exorcism, talking *directly* to the entity.

A few days later I decided to check Bonen. Sitting in my favorite chair in my living room, I took a deep breath to relax and to accumulate energy. To my astonishment, a foul odor assailed my nostrils; It smelled like human excretion and worse! Perplexed, I looked around me. I sniffed the air; there was nothing. Again, I took a deep breath and the same strong odor fairly choked me! I was startled. Then it came to me what was happening. I remembered a story of a similar situation told to me by the exorcist, Rev. Mat Hammer.

Hammer was requested to investigate a room where four persons over a period of years had committed suicide.

'When I arrived at the house,' Hammer related, 'I went directly up to the room, situated on the second floor, where the four people had killed themselves. The room was bare with but one window and a small closet.'

Then in a tone of incredulity he continued, 'In that room was the most horrible odor (See footnote) I've ever experienced! I flew out of there!' He explained, 'The terrible odor indicated the presence of a strong killer entity, extremely dangerous. I would have nothing more to do with it.'

Now I knew what I was up against. I was scared. Taking command of the situation, I shouted, 'Go with your guide to your next level of development!' At the same time I visualized a white light of protection about myself. The odor did not return. I assumed that the evil spirit had gone from the earth plane forever. I was badly mistaken.

During this period, my heart was a problem. If I became excited or physically too active, I would experience angina pain. The pain I experienced then was intense. It was mild compared to what happened next.

The next morning, shortly before awakening, I had a nightmare. A man with an evil and hateful look on his face came running straight toward me! I Instantly knew who he was. He was the same nasty character I had encountered the day before. In my sleep, I stood my ground but this time covered him with white light, a symbolic form of power. After awakening, I continued the projection of the light. 'That was the last time I saw him. My heart was pounding fast and the angina pain was almost unbearable. I survived. It was a severe lesson.

Footnote: When a person is attuned to the psychic, clairvoyance and clairaudience are possible. In this case the psychic sense of smell was stimulated. Dr. M. Scott Peck in his book *People of the Lie* also mentions the foul odor during some exorcisms.

Later, I was to exorcise a number of highly dangerous entities but by then I was wise enough to let my spirit friend, George, do the work. Some exorcists refer to such evil entities as demons. I do not. I think of them as highly intelligent, former living human beings who had failed to develop spiritually. They are of low morality. It is conceivable that they have been on the astral plane for thousands of years and have possessed many living persons. They have perpetrated their crimes time and time again. To rid this planet of such a scourge is the task for courageous and dedicated exorcists.

In the preceding chapters there has been much information given to enable the student of this work to have a clear understanding of why and how a possession occurs. In the following chapter a simplified and safe method of exorcism will be explained that is effective in clearing a person of undesirable spirit intruders. Such work is done at a distance, not in the presence of the client.

CHAPTER 9

The Clearing Process

The actual clearing or exorcism is relatively simple. When understanding the state of mind of the individual spirit entity (which is often a state of bewilderment) and understanding the laws of the spirit world which act upon him, a program can be designed to send him on his way. My program consists of five steps:

(1) By using the pendulum, I first determine if a subject is possessed. If so, I ask for the number of entities present and for the characteristics of the entities influencing the person.

(2) Through 'George,' a volunteer friend in the spirit world, I explain to the entities what has happened to them. I inform them that they are dead and do not belong to this earth plane. I make it clear to them that they are troublesome to themselves and to the subject and must leave.

(3) I then introduce each entity to a friendly spirit guide whom they see, recognize and trust. This spirit person may have been a friend, relative or teacher to the entity.

(4) I explain what will happen to the entities in their next plane of existence and development. The benefits and opportunities are stressed. They are asked to think about loved ones and friends who have died.

(5) Finally, I politely ask the entities to leave. If I suspect one is obstinate and does not want to leave, I put him into an

untenable position. Knowing that I can create any condition for him by visualization, he finds himself in a small cramped black box. He is then given the option to leave with the guide or stay in the box forever. He has really only one option.

The process of a clearing or exorcism is subject to the skill of the person doing the work. The laws governing the spirit world will suggest the right action to take. As the exorcist gains experience, improvements will be made in technique. There are no hard and fast rules to follow. One's successes will show the way.

I do not use the one-on-one method, pitting the exorcist against the invading spirit. I practice at a distance from the subject. I remain anonymous; the spirits know nothing about me.

The practicing exorcist should refrain from making an exorcism in the presence of the subject. This I cannot emphasize too strongly. Three very serious results may occur. First, the subject may suddenly be taken over by an invading spirit and become physically violent. Secondly, the spirit entity may size up the exorcist and decide to defy him and remain. Finally, more seriously, the exorcist may fall victim to the released spirit entity and become possessed!

MY METHOD OF CLEARING

I will now describe the method I use to exorcise a subject. The reader may wish to modify this method to one more suitable to his or her thinking and background. It may be shortened to save time. The process may be lengthened to include other desirable results. The wording may be changed. Although I avoid for the most part religious doctrine, the practitioner may feel more comfortable to include religious meaning in the ritual.

As this work requires concentration, I seat myself in a room where I will be undisturbed. Using a thought form in the shape of a circular wall, I mentally equate this as protection against any undesirable entity who may be present during the session. As previously mentioned, I had learned the hard way not to become involved with an unknown negative spirit entity. The first step in the process is to find the necessary information to evaluate the subject. One can do this by using the pendulum. The subconscious is used, not the conscious mind.

GETTING THE ANSWERS

To formulate a detailed evaluation of a subject, I use the form *Request for Healing and/or Clearing,* (Figure 3) which contain the essential personality questions requiring answers. Using the pendulum with Bill Finch's *Parametric Chart,* (Figure 2) I ask:

1. "Is this person possessed?" My pendulum will rotate in a clockwise direction if 'yes', or counterclockwise if 'no'.

2. If 'yes', I ask, "Give me an indication of the strongest possessing negative entity." The pendulum will swing to a negative number on the upper left section of the chart. The positive entities are of little concern at this point.

3. I follow with the question, "Give me an indication of the next strongest negative entity." I record my findings as I determine the characteristics of each possessing spirit entity in turn. When the pendulum swings to the vertical or neutral, there are no more possessing negative entities.

4. The catch-all question is asked. "Give me an indication of the total number of entities within and around this person." As the total is rarely over 100, I use the lower portion of the chart, 1 to 100.

5. Then I ask, "How many spirit entities reside in the person's home?" Using the lower section of the chart, 0 to 10, the pendulum will swing to the number.

6. It will take a few additional seconds to count the number of earthbound spirits at the person's place of work.

7. To determine the present health of a person, I ask, "Based on 100 percent being the best health this person has ever attained (usually at birth), what is his percentage of health now? Using the lower half of the chart as 0 to 100 percent, the pendulum will swing to his present health percentage. Health is very definitely tied in with possession. Almost always the health of a possessed person will be below 50 percent. When cleared, his/her health usually improves. (In Chapter 12 there is a brief explanation of spiritual healing.)

8. As there are negative influences acting upon a person, I ask, "How many negative energies has this person attracted?" Such dreaded energies are often called hexes. Again, I use the lower half of the chart, 0 to 10, to determine a quantity. A person with excellent health who is clear of entities, rarely has negative energies.A person who is experiencing a great deal of

personal trouble and hard times may have one or two.
(Chapter 11 deals with negative energies.)

9. Using the lower half of the chart, 0 to 100, I ask, "How
many negative programs of deprivation, anger and fear does
this person have?"

10. My final question is directed to the subject's higher
spiritual self, often call the High Self. "Do I have permission to
clear this person?" Usually, I get a 'yes' answer. In the event a
person is on trial for his life with a temporary insanity plea as
his defense, I refrain from performing an exorcism. After
clearing such a person, there would be little likelihood that he
could prove insanity in court. A guilty verdict may lead to his
execution.

It is my observation that in the majority of cases where
possession exists, the subject committed an act which invited
the entities to come aboard. The possession may have come
about by the subject becoming intoxicated with alcohol or
being blacked out using drugs. All too often the unwise delving
in the occult leads to entrapment by a devious and evil entity.

The question has been asked: If a person is possessed, why
doesn't a highly evolved spirit, who must be aware of the
condition, take corrective action on his own volition? Everyone
has free will to better or harm himself. There is every
indication that the subject has been responsible to some extent
in becoming possessed. Unless a living person asks help of the
spirit world for another, in this case for an exorcism, the spirit
guides will not intervene. When a living person asks the
subject's higher spiritual self for permission to help, that aid is
seldom refused. Can it be that we are truly our brother's
keeper?

We, as human beings, rarely exist as isolated individuals,
apart from others. People around us are constantly influencing
our thoughts, our behavior and our interaction with them. For
an exorcist, it is important, therefore to examine others around
the subject, his family and close associates. If any are
possessed, they also must be cleared. This can be time
consuming and mentally exhausting.

I take the position that not all possessing and vicinity spirit
entities are bad. In fact, they may be a loving relative. Most
entities are somewhat misguided but are not necessarily evil.
As I wish to be as helpful as I can, yet not too rough, I patiently
explain to the entity his circumstance and his options. After a

possessed person is identified, it is possible that the exorcism could be concluded by the guides without my help. I feel that I have accomplished something when I contribute to the process.

After determining the data given by the pendulum and observing the relationship existing between members of the same family circle, I am ready for the clearing.

To start the clearing process, I close my eyes and clairvoyantly see the face of a man who is my direct contact with the other side. He is the expert in the business of depossession. He may be one of my guides or guardian angels. I call him George, derived from the expression, "Let George do it!" He apparently knows what to do. He is there when I need him and I am thankful for his help. I speak to George as follows:

"Please address yourself to the earthbound spirit entities within the mind of (insert name), those around him, in his home and where he works. Please inform them that they are no longer of this earth plane. They are on the other side of the curtain called death. They feel very much alive and this is perfectly natural. Nevertheless, they do not belong here. They belong in a far better place. They are causing trouble to the person they are with as well as trouble to themselves. They must leave!"

BE GENTLE

At this point I start the process of persuading the earthbound spirits that leaving is a good thing for them. I speak to the entities - through George. My voice is gentle and sincere. The ritual of exorcism continues:

"Nearby each one of them is a friendly guide whom they recognize and trust. This guide will now take them to their next level of development and truth where they will be given healing, care, instruction and guidance, where their every need will be provided. Above all, they will be among those whom they love and who love them, those on the same side of the curtain of death as they are. Suggest to them, George, that they think about their loved ones, those who have died."

It should be noted how the laws of the spirit world are used. Any condition can be created for the spirit. A simple explanation of the spirit's situation was given. A guide was requested and introduced. Gentle persuasion was used when creating a 'Better Place.' At the instant he was asked to think about his loved ones, they appeared and whisked him away. In the event a spirit does not leave, I put him into a position so difficult that he has little option but to leave.

NOT WITH KID GLOVES

On occasion, an earthbound spirit may be reluctant to leave. He may also have no memory of anyone who loved him or whom he loved. He may even believe he is not dead! Now, to continue with the process of clearing:

At this point I toss away the cream and pour in the vinegar. I don't give a reluctant entity a choice. I throw him out! If I suspect that there are entities who did not leave, I change the tone of my voice to the timbre of a tough drill sergeant. Speaking in a harsh and uncompromising voice, I bark:

"For those of you who were so unwise as not to have accepted the terms just offered, or think you are not dead, you find yourselves in a small black, uncomfortable box with nails piercing it. You shall remain in that box, away from all human and living creatures, forever! This is so, unless and until you accept the terms just given you. Make up your mind: stay in the box or go with the guide. You have three seconds! One, two, three, go!"

Simultaneously to the three seconds warning, I take three deep breaths to accumulate energy which is released when I shout the word 'Go!' The disciples of Yoga and Huna put much emphasis on the intake of breath as a means of absorbing cosmic energy, called Prana and Mana, respectively. When the breath is exhaled, the energy is directed to accomplish a specific purpose. In this instance, it is used by the guides to do the work. I do not know if this ritual is absolutely necessary. It may not be, but since the process described here works, I continue to use it.

After this rough treatment, checking for entities is usually unnecessary as rarely any remain.

Remember, you can create any condition whatsoever for the entity. When he finds himself in the box he is uncomfortable and frightened. He wants to get out and will do as you say, especially if you don't give him time to think. Once he has made the decision to go with the guide, he has left this plane forever.

VAN DRIE'S CLEARING METHOD

Rev. John Van Drie uses a simplified approach to clear a person of invading entities. He equates asking the pendulum with asking the Superconscious for the answer. He made available to me the following procedure:

1. Use your pendulum with Bill Finch's Parametric chart. (Fig. 2)

2. Allow your pendulum to swing in the neutral or balance position. This is straight up and down. Ask if the subject is clear of spirit entities. If the answer is 'no', ask the pendulum to indicate the strongest negative one. Count each swing of the pendulum in the negative sector as a negative entity. When the pendulum finally swings back to the neutral position, ask if the subject has any positive entities on board. If the answer is 'yes', ask the pendulum to indicate the strongest positive one. Until the pendulum swings to the neutral position, count each swing in the positive sector as a positive entity. Record.

3. With the pendulum swinging in the neutral position, ask if the subject has any negative programs. If the pendulum swings into the negative range, count each swing as one program until the pendulum finally returns to the neutral position. Record.

4. Using your pendulum, ask if you have permission to clear the entities and negative programs. After getting a 'yes' answer, ask if the blanket of God's white light is around you. After again getting a 'yes' answer, you are ready for the clearing.

5. Say aloud or silently, "I now address the entities and negative programs in and around (subject's name and town). You are not of this world. You are on the other side of the veil called death. You will now find spirit guides standing beside you whom you love and trust. They will take you by the hand and lead you to your next level of spiritual development. As you feel the flow of energy passing through (subject's name) you will all leave." At this point, take several deep breaths and direct the pendulum to swing in a full clockwise motion. Then in a firm voice say, "Go!" Finally, relax, and watch the pendulum gradually return to the neutral position indicating all entities have left.

6. With your pendulum swinging in a clockwise direction, visualize a ten foot thick reflector placed around the subject.

Its surface reflects all evil back to its source in the form of love. Through this reflector, visualize love passing in either direction. Place a circle of fire around the subject so that no entities or negative programs can ever again penetrate to the heart of the subject. Finally, place enough guardian angels around the subject to enforce these conditions.

7. As a conclusion you may issue special instructions to your guides.

(a) If the subject was on alcohol or on drugs, direct the guides to remove any desire to use them.

(b) Direct love to flow to the subject from family members and all persons with whom he or she comes in contact. Open the subject to the feeling of love for all people.

(c) Give special directions for health, happiness, contentment and harmony.

Even though Rev. Van Drie's method differs markedly from the method I advocate, his method produces excellent results. The bottom line is that a clearing can be accomplished by using any number of methods. It can be as complicated or as simple as the person doing the clearing wishes to make it. As the person gains experience, problems not related to possession such as negative programs and negative energies, can be successfully identified and neutralized.

MASS CLEARINGS

After a person learns to use the pendulum, he may ask how many earthbound spirits are there in a particular cemetery or in an old church. Hundreds reside in such places. Thousands more live within the ocean depths where ships have sunk. Hospitals and prisons are prime targets for an exorcist. Unlimited power is at the disposal of the person conducting a clearing; he can clear the whole lot at the same time! As an exorcist services more requests for a clearing, the workload will require him to group people in a single exorcism. Such 'production' methods work just as well as a single one.

The limitation to a group clearing is that oftentimes there may be certain individuals who require special attention. There is a tendency to miss the special requirements, such as treatment for abstaining alcohol or using drugs. Also, it may be wise to treat a single evil entity, a potential murderer, with a little more caution. You may wish to be more personal and gentle with the spirit of a close relative, such as a parent of the possessed person.

SELF-CLEARING

How can you tell if negativity is directed toward you or if there is a negative spirit bothering you? It really depends upon your disposition. Let us say for example, you are normally a contented person, not easily disturbed with conditions around you. Then for no apparent reason you find yourself irritable and out of sorts. This may be caused by a foreign influence. If you compare your disposition a year or month ago and find it changed for the worse, this may give you a clue to what is wrong.

The question is asked, "If I should feel a presence around me, can I exorcise myself?" The answer is yes even if you are not certain there are spirits near you. I recommend the following simple procedure. First, find a place where you will be undisturbed. Assume there is a competent guide nearby who knows all about removing unwanted spirit entities. Say aloud, "Friendly spirit guide, remove the spirits near me and send them to where they need to go. Thank you."

Any nearby spirits will leave. If there had been a negative spirit interfering with you, you will feel an immediate uplifting in disposition.

Even with my normally positive attitude, I too, occasionally get caught up in a negative mood. Usually I do not detect the change or realize what is happening until someone close to me will point out what I am saying or doing. It is then that I take the appropriate action. Within minutes, I return to my normal self.

Health is another matter. Even a friendly spirit, who died of an illness, can bring that particular illness to you. It is simply unwise to attract any discarnate spirit to you. Should there be one near you, lovingly ask it to leave.

Finally, if you determine that you have been unsuccessful in clearing yourself, request an exorcist to do the work for you. The exorcism may be done in your presence or at a distance.

THE LESSON

There is a mountain of evidence that the spirits who wander in the astral plane were never informed about what would happen to them after they died. Very often their beliefs when alive conflict with their findings after dying. They do not know what to believe. They are confused and lost.

It does not take a special talent to clear persons of spirit possession. The most important requirement is to have the desire to do the work. Specialized knowledge of what happens in the spirit world is essential, because the action occurs there. It is helpful to use the pendulum, as it is an effective tool to contact the subconscious of the subject. On the other hand, observation combined with a keen intuition, can detect possession. **A possessed person has three striking characteristics. He is extremely negative in his thinking, his behavior is markedly antisocial and he is deeply depressed.**

Should the number of intruding spirits not be known, the exorcist will not have a problem clearing any who may be present. One, or a hundred, may be dispatched at the same time. This will include both negative and positive entities, as neither have any business interfering with the personality of the subject.

Although you may not be aware of any spirit helpers about you, they are there waiting to be helpful. As many of our problems in the real world are caused by spirit interference, our helpers can be of immense help in removing the cause of such trouble. Skeptics have asked these unseen beings for help in clearing others and then to their amazement have found the job done. After several such experiences, there are few skeptics.

In conclusion, it should be emphasized that there is no one set ritual or method in performing an exorcism. You can devise a procedure which suits your background and beliefs. It is advisable to perform the clearing at a distance. A face-to-face meeting with a possessed person during an exorcism can be physically dangerous, or stressful at the least. Let a knowledgeable spirit guide on the other side do the work. Instruct the guide to send the intruding spirits to a place of no return. You need not even have to believe that such a guide exists. Be confident that your request was fulfilled. It is not necessary to be a psychic and to know exactly what occurs. The results are what counts.

It is unnecessary to convince anyone about the validity of the work that you are doing, and you need not explain. Do the work alone in the quiet of your room. Ask clear and concise questions of your pendulum. Use your judgment and ingenuity to seek out causes. Based on a sound understanding of this work, take the appropriate action.

Should your subject attract a whole new set of entities after your initial success in removing the first group, you are blameless. You may, of course, wish to be of further help. You can clear the subject again and continue to search for the cause of the attraction by an undesirable spirit. Often, the second clearing allows the subject to have a second chance at controlling and understanding his mixed up emotions. Continuation of your efforts to help is aided by the cooperation and feedback from the person making the initial request.

Distance plays no part in the clearing process. You may clear a person half way around the world and be as effective as if that person were in your immediate vicinity. Half of the some 3000 persons I cleared in the past seven years lived outside of the Chicago area where I reside, some as far as Australia and India. You are working in the spirit world where time and distance have no meaning. In addition, with the knowledge that you have gained in this book, you can have instant communication with any spirit that you need to reach.

Limitations to this work are those you place on yourself. The knowledge of clearing a person of spirit possession at a distance can be used as an awesome creative tool. In the next chapter you will gain an insight into the vast possibilities of using an exorcism to drastically alter adverse social and world situations for the better.

CHAPTER 10

The
Criminal Mind

The skill of performing an exorcism can be very useful when dealing with the criminal element or with violent persons. Severe and violent situations can be reversed by concentrating on the individuals involved. The following cases illustrate the magic one can create using ingenuity and a little effort.

THE GANG

In Chicago there are neighborhood organizations dedicated to reporting suspicious situations and crime to the police department. I am a member of one such organization and my contact is Police Officer Ann Frank. Recently she expressed frustration with a situation.

"This lady has been calling me two of three times every week for the past three weeks." Ann related, "There's a gang of young men who are terrorizing both her and her teen-age son. She's terribly afraid and has asked for police protection."

"I think I can do something about that." I said, "Let me have the names of the gang members and I'll work on them. I will need only the first names and ages, if you have them."

"Yes, here they are," replied Ann, "There are nine in all. Anything you can do will be appreciated."

I pocketed the list and upon leaving, said, "Let me know what happened."

That evening I carefully diagnosed the personality characteristics of the young men. Five were possessed and all had serious domestic and psychological problems. A clearing was performed and a treatment for harmony was given to each in the group. Three weeks later I returned to Ann's office.

"Have I got something to tell you!" She greeted me. I smiled, "Hope it's interesting. Is it about the gang?"

"Yes," She replied, "let me tell you how unexpectedly everything turned out. A day or two after I saw you, the mother and her son were walking down the street when they were approached by one of the gang members. This man had been particularly violent and threatening to the woman. When she saw him, she fled. The son stayed and talked to the young man. Later, the son told his mother, 'That fellow couldn't understand why you ran away, mom, all he wanted was to be my friend.' There's been no more trouble," Ann concluded.

THE CULT BUILDER

I have always been intrigued with new ideas, especially those with a challenge. Some years ago our company gave a job to a parolee named Scotty after he had been released from Joliet State Penitentiary. He had served 8 years of a 10 year sentence for armed robbery. Scotty had committed 150 armed holdups, specializing in taverns. He had also stolen over a hundred automobiles. He only stole Pontiacs. He explained his preference, "In a Pontiac, I could always outrun the cops."

Scotty had been caught and convicted for only five hold-ups. He deplored the verdict and sentence as being unfair for just five hold-ups! Scotty was a likable fellow but was somewhat of a con-artist. After a few years of freedom, he slipped back into his old ways. He was apprehended and sentenced to serve another 10 years, this time at Joliet Correctional Institute.

Back in prison, Scotty had time and opportunity to plan and scheme for that day when again he would be free. His plan was on a grandiose scale. Now at the age of 39 he had become a prolific writer with considerable charm. One letter to me would often take a half hour to read. His letters outlined plan after plan. His main direction was working with women. He had somehow found the names of some fifty women and was molding their thinking in a specific direction: to serve him upon his release. His basic plan was to create a cult organization, with himself at the head. The income of these women was to be channeled to him and invested in numerous enterprises he had conceived. These enterprises consisted of a high production chicken farm, a studio to reproduce paintings, an export-import company and numerous others. He had established some of these companies on paper and was selling shares while still in prison!

Each succeeding letter gave further evidence that the details of his plans were being well formulated. There was a good chance of success. As his approach to each venture had an element of chicanery, I became concerned. It was then that I began my investigation of Scotty's personality by using the pendulum. I asked questions which could be answered with a yes or no swing.

Not surprisingly, I discovered that three spirit entities were directing Scotty's mind and a dozen or so were near him. Scotty was possessed. The spirit intruders were promptly sent on their way. Shortly afterwards the tone of his letters abruptly changed. Scotty began to talk more about practical plans, ideas based on sound business principles. Gone were his fantasies, the kingdom and harem of beautiful and obedient women! More important, the air of deceit was no longer present.

After serving five years on the second sentence, Scotty was again released and put on parole. For a year or so after his freedom, he did odd jobs for our company. Gradually he accumulated enough capital to go into business for himself.

Today, Scotty is a well-established and successful business man. His resourcefulness and imagination have created a unique method for processing food for tropical fish. True, handsome Scotty still has a fascination for a pretty face, but no longer is there larceny in his every project.

My friendship with Scotty gave birth to many possibilities. Would it be possible to influence the minds of other criminals? Could their anti-social behavior be changed and their criminal activity stopped? Subsequent experiments proved most productive.

WHO IS THE MURDERER?

We often read in the newspapers stories of a murder or what may be described as a series of murders. Almost invariably, when making a personality analysis of the criminal who committed these crimes, (it is not necessary to identify him by name) he is spirit possessed. Furthermore, the spirit entities directing his mind will most often measure -20 to -30 on the *Parametric Scale*. A -20 individual is a dangerous criminal who will kill with provocation or under duress. A -30 personality is an extremely dangerous criminal who has the compulsion to kill without motive or provocation. Refer to Bill Finch's yardstick of personality analysis described in Chapter 7 for a more complete description of these characteristics.

Even though a criminal has not been identified, nor his whereabouts known, he may still be cleared. After the clearing, it is interesting to note what happens. There will be few, if any, reports of crimes attributed to that particular individual. He may simply disappear leaving no further trace. On the other hand, the criminal may let his guard down allowing himself to be captured. Such occurred in the following case.

COLEMAN-BROWN, KILLERS

Authorities had identified Alton Coleman and his girl friend, Debra Brown, as participants in a six-state crime spree, which included assault, rape, kidnaping and murder. On checking Coleman for possession, I found he was controlled by a dangerous -25 entity and had an additional 24 entities nearby. Brown was possessed, but not as severely as Coleman. Both were then exorcised at a distance.

Two days later both Coleman and Brown were captured without resistance. Without apparent reason, they had simply returned to their old neighborhood where they were immediately recognized and apprehended.

At their hearing, both Coleman and Brown pleaded innocent. From every indication, the real Coleman and real Brown may indeed be innocent. In my opinion the controlling immoral entities, to a large extent, were responsible. In all likelihood the two could vaguely, if at all, recall their deeds. Returning to their home and not evading capture would indicate ignorance of their crimes.

A jury found both Coleman and Brown guilty of first degree murder. Both face execution.

THE THREE FACES OF NANCY

More frequently than is commonly known, a person gets in serious trouble when a second personality takes control of the person's mind and body. The following story of Nancy Clark is the tragic result of such possession. The article below, written by Susan Jimison, appeared in *Weekly World News*, May 27, 1986.

"Nice Nancy Clark was a mild mannered mom, a church-going housewife and a pillar of the community - until another personality took over her body and she wound up in jail for the rest of her life.

"Eventually doctors discovered that the Marietta, Georgia, woman had three separate personalities, a case reminiscent of the 1957 Joanne Woodward film, *Three Faces of Eve.*

"Last year she went on a rampage and committed 17 felonies ranging from armed robbery to arson and kidnapping. She was sentenced to 165 years in prison for the crimes, which experts say were masterminded by Nanna, one of her multiple personalities."

Susan Jimison reported that Mrs. Clark, 32, was essentially a well-bred lady, a church leader and the mother of an 8-month old baby. Her psychologist, Dr. George B. Greaves could not understand at first why such a model citizen would go on such an illogical criminal rampage. The circumstance of the crime as well as the lack of a rational motive convinced the doctor that she was a victim of multiple personalities.

"The plump brunette's crime spree involved two incidents, one on July 2, 1985, and one on August 19, 1985. Police say she disguised herself and robbed her victims at gunpoint.

"In the first incident she entered the home of elderly neighbors, robbed them and forced them to drive to their bank and withdraw $1,100. She then returned the old couple to their home, taped them up and set fire to their basement. Fortunately, the victims escaped without harm from their burning home.

"In the second incident, Mrs. Clark held up an elderly man and his son after talking her way into their home. She forced the pair to drive to their credit union and, while the younger man went inside to negotiate the withdrawal of $1,500, she held the old man hostage.

"The son called the police and Mrs. Clark was captured.

"Only after Mrs. Clark had confessed to the crimes and been sent to prison did suspicions arise that she might be suffering from multiple personalities.

"Dr. Greaves confirmed her condition by hypnotizing her and speaking first to a 5-year-old personality named Nickie and then to a sinister woman named Nanna."

The doctor reported, 'Nickie told me Nancy was molested at five by a neighbor. Then came Nanna who claims to be in her 20's, but she reacts in a very childlike way. Nanna is petulant and angry and thinks she's Nancy's sister. She was annoyed with Nancy for never having any adventures. She was searching for adventure and thought it would be great good fun to go out and rob people. She felt this was a game she was playing.'

When Dr. Greaves asked Nanna how it felt when she got caught, she replied, 'I didn't, Nancy did.'

"In her April trial, a jury ruled that Mrs. Clark was guilty but mentally ill.

"She's in prison now - and Nickie and Nanna are right there with her." (See footnote)

Obviously, the medical profession is giving second thoughts to the problems associated with multiple personalities. We can but speculate that there were many persons convicted and imprisoned due to the nefarious guidance of an intelligent alien entity. We can expect to see more attention being paid by progressive psychologists to criminals suspected of multiple personalities disorder (MPD).

THE NIGHT STALKER

During a lecture tour in California in 1985 I heard a short news report of a killer on the loose. He was labeled the Night Stalker as most of his crimes were committed at night. His mode of operation was to invade his victim's home at night. His target was usually a young woman. He raped and killed without pity.

When speaking before an audience of about 60 people, I

(Footnote) An analysis I made indicated that Nanna measured -18 in the Parametric Chart and Nickie +5. I sent both to another dimension. As Nancy was fortunately sent to a mental institution and not to a prison, a mental improvement will some day allow her to be set free.

asked for further information about the killer. I was informed that he was responsible for the murder of 14 young women. At the last report he was operating in the nearby Los Angeles area. He had not yet been identified.

I decided to stop the killer. Also, the demonstration would provide further proof of the effectiveness of my methods. Using my pendulum, I discovered two -25 negative entities controlling the Night Stalker. Either one of these vicious spirits was capable of the crimes attributed to the killer.

In front of my audience I then performed the distant exorcism. Afterwards, the pendulum indicated that the man was clear of intruding spirits. I concluded with the statement, "This man is no longer capable of committing murder. He shortly will be captured or will disappear, not to be heard of again."

A few days after the exorcism, the Night Stalker was identified as Richard Ramirez, a 25-year old drifter from El Paso, Texas. His picture was also published in the newspapers. Two weeks after my demonstration, Ramirez tried to steal a car in broad daylight. He was immediately recognized by the owner of the car, a young lady. She shouted for help. Her neighbors came running to her aid. They pursued Ramirez and caught him. When they realized who the man was they beat him unmercifully. If the police had not intervened, Ramirez would have certainly been beaten to death.

Although Ramirez was alleged to have committed other felonies after the exorcism, there is no evidence that he committed another murder. I believe that when the intelligent criminal spirits left, the killer no longer had their cunning to guide him. He then fell easy prey to his captors.

The obvious purpose of clearing an unknown criminal, one who is making the headlines, is to stop his criminal activity. As for me, apprehension or incarceration, possibly execution, is not the objective. The cessation of his further criminal acts is. An analogy suggests itself from a personal experience.

During World War II, I was an artillery forward observer. My objective, when directing artillery fire was not to kill enemy soldiers. It was to neutralize them, to prevent them from taking action against us. For example, if the enemy was directing artillery at us, it was sufficient to fire in the general vicinity of his observer. Without his direction, the guns fell silent. In war as with crime, revenge is purposeless. To stop a person from further violence is what matters. Effective deterrent also can be applied to those recently released from prison.

PAROLE OFFICER, SKEPTIC

A friend of the family is a parole officer. He is also a cynic and does not buy all that 'spirit talk.' After some persuasion, and perhaps to humor me, he gave me his list of parolees to check for possession. The last name of each person was omitted. Later in the quiet of my study, using the pendulum, I carefully checked each name on the list. Of the 181 persons checked, male and female, 94 were possessed or 52%. Of the group possessed there were 5 very dangerous criminals. Any one of them, if he thought he could get away with it, would have satisfaction in murdering the parole officer! The possessed group was exorcised. A month later they were rechecked and found to be still clear with the exception of 7 persons who were then again exorcised.

Several months later, the parole officer, no longer a diehard skeptic, handed me his current list. "What d'ya know," He greeted me with a grin, "I'm the only parole officer in the state without a repeater!" He added, "Not one of my people broke his parole."

When you learn to perform an exorcism at a distance, you may desire to scan the newspapers and clear the murderers, rapists, burglars and other odd criminals on the loose. You should use caution, nevertheless, as you will be releasing highly dangerous and intelligent spirit beings. You must be confident such spirits will be directed to a place where they can do no further harm.

You need not confine your activity to exorcising criminals. You can take a look at world affairs and use your knowledge there. Often persons who perform notorious acts are possessed by evil entities directing those acts. By clearing such people who may be possessed, their harmful thinking ceases. They no longer wish to continue their injurious activity. The following story illustrates how you can defuse a dangerous situation.

THE HIJACKERS

In November, 1984, a group of desperadoes seized a Kuwait airliner in flight and directed it to land at the airport in Teheran, Iran. When the plane landed at the Teheran airport, the terrorists demanded that Kuwait release seven of their imprisoned comrades. The Kuwait government refused. The hijackers began to kill the passengers. Two Kuwait and two United States citizens were subsequently murdered. The desperadoes threatened to kill another man each day until their demands were met.

At the time, I was visiting the home of Dr. Marcus Bach, author and popular lecturer. Dr. Leonid Kovalevsky, aerospace structure research specialist, accompanied me. During our visit, the subject of the hijack came up. Apparently, subconsciously, I had been giving the highly explosive situation some thought. Without a moment's hesitation, I exclaimed, "I almost forgot, I should have taken care of that situation!" I added, I'll do it this evening." I knew that I had the key to the solution.

Later that evening, when Leonid and I were having dinner, I reasoned: "There has to be a person among the hijackers who is possessed by a strong killer entity. If not, there would be no killings." After making this comment, I asked, "I wonder how many hijackers there are?" There had been no reports of how many persons had commandeered the airliner. I then assigned letters to the hijackers from 'A' to 'H', the leader being 'A'. I swung my pendulum over the Parametric Chart and began to diagnose each man. The leader 'A' was not possessed. The second man 'B' had a strong -20 entity on board. He was the killer. 'C' had a minor negative entity and was not a killer. 'D' was clear. There were no more men; only four in all. (This later proved to be correct.)

At the dinner table that evening I exorcised the hijackers. Then I closed my eyes and visualized in my mind the hijackers being in harmony with the remaining passengers. Earlier, the women and children had been released. I also visualized the hijackers being in harmony with the crew members and with all persons outside the aircraft who had anything to do with them. The entire procedure took about ten minutes.

The next morning the news media reported that the hijackers were subdued without a struggle by police posing as aircraft maintenance men. As the Iranian government condoned the aircraft take-over, the hijackers were whisked away and were never heard of again.

A short time later, another aircraft was hijacked. A quick pendulum analysis and exorcism followed. The incident immediately closed without violence.

Whether or not the exorcisms had anything to do with the peaceful conclusions of the hijack incidents will never be known. Exorcising persons in similar situations may prove fruitful in resolving dangerous crises in the future. The following series of events illustrates how an exorcism can have far reaching results.

TERRORISM

By exorcising a person in high office, such as a president, king or ruler, who may be spirit possessed, astonishing results often take place. The exorcism of President Muammar Khadafy of Libya is a case in point. Here is the story.

On December 27, 1986, a radical Palestinian terrorist group made two devastating attacks on the Rome and Vienna airports. 19 people were killed, many of whom were women and children. In addition, 80 persons were injured, some seriously. The attacks were aimed at the Israeli El Al Airline check-in counters.

A few days later the newspaper, Chicago Sun Times, reported: "In Tripoli, the government of radical Arab leader Muammar Khadafy called the airport assaults 'heroic' and 'brave' actions, the official news agency JANA said." It was Libya's first comment on the attacks.

Khadafy had long supported the Palestinians in their struggle against the Israelis. His government had openly aided the terrorist group which had launched the attacks. For this attack the United States and Israel vowed to take strong counter-measures against Libya.

Libyan strongman Muammar Khadafy had frequent clashes with the United States, as well as with his neighboring countries. Born in 1942, the son of desert nomads, Khadafy was raised as a fundamentalist Moslem. He was educated in Britain at Sandhurst Military Academy before returning to Libya in 1966 as a member of the army. Khadafy took power in 1969 by leading a successful coup against King Idris.

Based on the premise that it was not natural to approve wanton killings, I speculated that Khadafy could possibly be possessed. On January 4th I checked him for possession. He was indeed possessed. A few moderately strong negative entities were in control. The strongest was rated -15. (Refer to Chapter 7) None could commit murder. Khadafy was exorcised. I then told my associate, John Van Drie, "Now watch the change come over Khadafy. He will completely reverse his stand on the raids."

Six days later, on January 10th the Christian Science Monitor reported: "Khadafy (Qaddafi), Reversing Himself, Condemns Airport Terrorists." The report was written in Tripoli, Libya. It continued, "In a 180 degree reversal of his previous statements, Col.Muammar Khadafy, the Libyan leader, condemned the men who attacked the Rome and Vienna airports as 'completely mad.' He pledged to fight terrorism, Western diplomats said yesterday. According to Western European diplomats who attended a rare meeting with Colonel Khadafy Wednesday night, the Libyan leader said he was trying to discourage Palestinians from attacking targets outside Israel and Israeli-occupied areas."

The article in the Monitor concluded with the statement: "Khadafy's comments contrasted sharply with earlier remarks in which he praised the Palestinian gunmen who assulted the Rome and Vienna airports with grenades and submachine guns on December 27th."

Apparently something has happened to Khadafy as 36 months have since gone by without a substantiated report that his country has been linked with any terrorist operation.

There is no need to be concerned if a world leader is not possessed and an exorcism ritual is performed. If there are no invading spirits, nothing is accomplished, good or bad. No changes will occur. Should we believe that the action a particular world leader is taking is wrong and possibly evil, it does not necessarily follow that the person is possessed.

Basically, spirits who possess the living are of low moral character and have little spiritual awareness. Should such spirits interfere with a prominent public figure, their removal can only benefit the person as well as the society which he governs. The exorcist removes problem creating entities.

The practitioner of exorcism cannot direct the person or the entities to create additional mischief beyond that which they are already capable of doing.

A MORAL PROBLEM?

If a crime is committed while the subject is possessed by an evil spirit entity, who is guilty? Who should be punished, the subject or the intruder? As a practical matter, the spirit goes free and the subject takes the rap, even up to the death penalty. Occasionally, a defendant is judged temporarily insane and thereby escapes severe punishment for his act.

The moral question arises: should the living person pay the penalty for an act dictated by another? How many more Miskomens are serving life terms or have been executed? (See Chapter 2) As noted in the survey of parolees, 94 of 181 were possessed. Just who was responsible for their antisocial behavior? What would happen if every parolee is exorcised when leaving prison?

Referring to the Coleman-Brown case, what caused the two to return to their former habitat where they were readily recognized and just as easily apprehended? Was it that they were no longer controlled by vicious entities? I question whether Coleman could explain his criminal acts. More than likely he could not even recall them.

Acts of violence committed by a person possessed by strong evil minded spirits, cast serious doubts on the moral justification of the death penalty. The situation urgently cries aloud for further study of multiple personalities, both to help prevent crime and to help a criminal cease his unlawful behavior. From my observation, I find that very few persons, after having been cleared of spirit possession, will return to their former antisocial conduct. From every indication, a comprehensive investigation in this field of inquiry could well produce a breakthrough in relieving our society of much of the crime we are experiencing today.

A frequently asked question is, 'What is the moral responsibility of an exorcist when he clears a person without his permission?' There are two parts to the answer. First of all, every person has free will. A possessing spirit is interfering with that free will. It is a case where an intelligent alien entity is imposing its will over the will of the subject. It is an invasion of privacy; it is one person controlling or enslaving another. Even when the possessing spirit is a good spirit, it has no right to direct the activities of the host body. The second part of the answer is more subtle. In the process of an exorcism, the exorcist is presumably in touch with the subject's Superconscious or High Self. The pendulum is used. Permission for the clearing is requested. Seldom is it refused.

Caution should be used when a criminal is apprehended and is found possessed. Should the exorcist clear him at once? If the defendant has a plea of temporary insanity - possession can be just that - the exorcist can endanger his plea. If he is cleared before the trial, a competent psychologist could prove him sane. A guilty verdict may mean his execution.

Clearing a possessed person sentenced for execution and who has little likelihood of being declared mentally ill and reprieved, will insure that the vicious controlling entities will no longer be set free after the death of the host body. When the intruding entities are sent to a place of no return, there will be fewer malevolent spirits around to perpetuate their wicked crimes on another potential victim.

THE KILLER WITHIN

A characteristic of possession is that all too often the possessing entity tries to kill or injure the host body. For example, a child will strike his head on a wall in anger or bash his fist through a door. The extreme is when the subject attempts suicide without obvious or known reason. Where there is a strong, evil entity in control, the person may commit a number of violent crimes without apparent concern for self-protection. It is as if the person wishes to be caught and to suffer the consequence of his misdeeds. The Coleman-Brown crime spree may have been such a case.

It invariably follows that the innate cruelty of a strong, immoral entity will wish his host to suffer. From my experience, I know that those persons who can 'hear' the entity speak, will often report how abusive the language is. Such a possessing spirit will typically tell his host, "You're rotten; you can't do anything right! You're ugly; nobody could possibly love you!" Or the possessed person will hear, "You're useless, kill yourself! Take an overdose of sleeping pills, it's easy." For a person inclined to believe a spirit can solve all his problems, he may hear, "As your Spirit Master, I command you to prepare yourself to commit suicide on March 15th!"

I can only speculate why an entity would wish his host to die. The entity apparently finds himself trapped and wishes to get out. The entity who wanted to enjoy the experiences of another living body had little trouble getting in; he has difficulty getting out. An analogy of the convict can be used. Through his ignorance and harmful intent, he was imprisoned. Now, he cannot find the key to escape. For some reason the invading spirit becomes tired of living in the body he has chosen. There may be other entities present giving him competition for control. He may be disillusioned living in a particular body. He wants out. When he finally does free himself and is able to attach himself to the next victim of his choosing, the process undoubtedly begins all over again.

THE SUICIDAL PERSONALITY

Although there is insufficient data on persons who have suicidal tendencies, the few I have checked were possessed. It is often true that a person who is possessed loses the will to live and will do something which will lead to his death.

A spirit entity who had little value for life when on earth will have the same disregard for the life of the host body. An entity measuring -20 to -30 on the Parametric Scale will frequently try to convince his host to commit suicide. When I detect such strong negative entities on a person, I can say with some certainty that the person has suicidal tendencies. Often my diagnosis is confirmed.

A young man of my acquaintance, age 20, in a moment of deep depression let his auto engine run in a closed garage. Asphyxiation caused his death. Some time later the young man was able to communicate with his father through a trance medium. When he was asked why he killed himself he could offer no explanation and expressed deep remorse. He had led an intemperate life and more than likely had been possessed, yet was never aware of it.

We are faced at this time with a serious problem among our teenagers. The suicide rate has drastically escalated during the past 10 years. During this same period the use of non-prescription drugs by this age group has also increased. *All too often possession occurs by using drugs. The conclusion is clear: The intemperance use of drugs will attract intelligent evil entities who often urge the drug abuser to commit suicide. The victim will frequently succeed in killing himself or attempt suicide without any logical reason for doing so.*

When a person succeeds in taking his life, his problems are not over. Charles Hampton in his book, *The Transition Called Death*, addresses himself to this problem: (pp. 78-79)

"If a man has given way to drink on earth, and is now earth-bound, he will try to smell and taste liquor by possessing a drinker, thus achieving a vicarious satisfaction. There would be a good deal less drinking, over-eating and sexual excess if people could see the thirsty 'dead drunks' hanging around bars, and see the libertines seeking sensuous satisfaction through the bodies of others.

"One ought to be fairly free from temptation to undertake to help a suicide. Often, when a suicide has attached himself to a living person, he complains. 'I can't get rid of that gross fellow!' He imagines the living person is possessing him! In many ways, it is a fifty-fifty proposition and requires a strong will by the living to break it. Unfortunately, often such people are weak-willed. The possessing connection can be broken by an exorcism. Ultimately, each person must develop his own will power to be master of his body."

Hampton concludes his remarks, "Since the departed live in a world of thought and feeling, the important help we can give is uplifting love, emotion, and the calm power of thought."

A CHALLENGE

We must ask ourselves: If a spirit entity is instrumental in causing the death of one person, how many more deaths has he caused over the thousands of years he may have been acting on this plane? How many more deaths will he cause in the future? As a final solution, it becomes absolutely necessary that the released entity be dispatched to a place where he can do no further harm. An exorcism conducted correctly, does exactly that.

With the skill that you have acquired in clearing persons of spirit possession, you can affect the outcome of world events. Even if you do not operate on an international scale, you can stop desperate criminals or prevent potential suicides. The newspapers are full of such material. Keep a pencil and pad handy. Jot down the names of persons involved in questionable activities. Later, at your leisure, check them for entities and if possessed, clear them. Not often will you get feed back for your efforts. You need only a few successful known results to be richly rewarded.

By our understanding of the spirit world and the methods that we now can use, we have a powerful tool to help people. There are other tools, however, just as effective to alter the life of man. In the next chapter we will discuss the power projected by our thoughts, positive and negative.

CHAPTER 11
Picturization

Students of metaphysics know that visualization is a powerful tool used in the process of creating anything. It is recognized that before anything can come into being it must first be created in the mind. The word 'Picturization' was coined by Harold Sherman to describe controlled visualization.

VISUALIZATION AND THOUGHT-FORMS

Much has been written about thought-forms, how they are created, their multipurpose uses and their effectiveness. A thought-form is thought energy. It is produced by one's thoughts. The more energy given such thoughts, the stronger the thought-form.

A thought-form can be shaped by the hands into objects with dimensions. Although invisible to most people, it can be seen by a few clairvoyants. With a little practice, almost everybody can feel one. As an example of what they are, the following amusing story illustrates a practical use for them.

SEEING IS BELIEVING

During a healing lecture in London one evening, a portly woman in her mid-fifties, kept interrupting the lecturer with questions and statements of opinions, all alluding to her gifts as a psychic. I concluded that she was on an ego trip and mentally made a note to have nothing to do with her.

After the session, as I walked to my quarters, I observed her walking about thirty feet behind me. Again, I reminded myself to keep my distance 'from that nut.' At that moment she loosened a verbal barrage in my direction, hurling insults and threats at me. I was startled. I had never spoken to her and had but glanced at her in the darkness.

After a moment of perplexity, it suddenly occurred to me what was happening. She was reading my mind! I snapped my brain to attention, and immediately visualized a red brick wall, a thought form, directly behind me, between myself and the woman. When I did this she was directing a string of choice superlatives in my direction. In the middle of the sentence she abruptly stopped. With a smile, I glanced back at her. Her mouth was still open; her expression was one of shock! Not another word was uttered. Perhaps she was the world's greatest psychic. Did she see the wall?

After I had demonstrated thought-forms to my inquisitive dentist, Dr. Vincent Biank, he and his two children had a great time with them. Using the hands, one would create a thought-form shape, such as a cube, ball or cone, and the other two would feel it and guess its shape. Vince proudly declared his score was four out of six. The children did better, he admitted.

A thought-form can be used to influence the thinking and action of others, often without their knowledge. In Dr. Peter Albright's book, *Body, Mind and Spirit,* Dr. Edward Jastram makes this observation on thought-forms. (p. 238)

"Other forms of invasion may be described as obsessions which if energetic and structured enough, may be called thought-forms. These take on certain aspects of personality and may be treated as such. That is to say, they appear to show initiative and purpose in a limited way. They can cause confusion and problems of the mind and body similar to the effects of entities. Obsessions and thought-forms were brought to light as possible parts of a problem when it was found that eliminating entities did not always solve the problems of the host."

NEGATIVE ENERGIES

Have you ever walked into a room where two or more people were having a violent argument and felt the tension, not only existing between the antagonists, but in the room itself? Have you perchance gone to an ancient ruin and felt depressed with what you saw? Have you been with a person who simply radiated negativity to such an extent that you could hardly wait to flee from his or her presence? Have you heard the expression, 'It is not a happy house'? In such a house people feel uncomfortable, yet from all outward appearances the physical attraction of the building may be superior. What we have in each of these examples is an intuitive sense that something is wrong. We may become depressed even to the extent that we carry away that feeling for several days afterwards. We are sensing the energy of a negative thought form.

When expressing an emotion with great feeling, there is a release of energy. It is analogous to a puff of smoke, smoke which may stay in place for hundreds of years. One can not see it but it is there waiting to permeate the mind of any who pass. Dr. Jastram has a name for it. He calls such energies Vritties, a Sanskrit word meaning thought-forms or thought energies.

Vritties of a negative nature are especially strong in such places as the former Nazi concentration camps. A sensitive person is repelled by the dreadful atmosphere of these prisons. So much misery, hate and unbridled emotions have impinged the air and even the ground with the darkest vibrations of savagery. If ever an area needed neutralizing, these former prisons should have priority.

We are concerned with dispelling negative vritties as they cause so much turmoil and tragedy in the world about us.

Walter H. Woods in his talk before the American Society of Dowsers 1985 Convention in California spoke about negative thought forces as being equally detrimental as possession.

"There are other areas you can deal with, such as negative psychic influences. Frequently, there is a need to block them off. Energy sapping is such an area. You may examine a person and find that he has been sapped of energy six or seven times. He complains that he is always worn out. Blocking can be accomplished by shielding, a mental projection of protection from detrimental or inharmonious conditions. Such shielding is used for psychic, mental, physical, noxious, or satanic blocking. On the other hand, care must be used as often the person doing the sapping vitally needs that energy. He may be ill and the energy aids in his recovery."

To these thoughts, Dr. Carl Wickland, in his book *Thirty Years Among the Dead*, (p. 17) speaks of the negative energy imparted to the living by the dead.

"Humanity is surrounded by the thought influence of millions of discarnated beings, who have not yet arrived at a full realization of life's higher purposes. A recognition of this fact accounts for a great portion of unbidden thoughts, emotions, outbursts of temper, strange foreboding, uncontrollable infatuations and countless other mental vagaries."

ANCIENT SPELLS

Negative energies, whether caused by a living person or disembodied entity, are first cousins to story book curses and spells of ancient times. The practice of cursing or making a spell using imagery with a forceful display of energy was recorded in Scotland in the 16th Century. *Spiegelschrift* (p. 378)

"Those who had seen old women, of the Madge Wildfire School, cursing and shrieking, say their manner is well calculated to inspire terror. Some fifteen or twenty years ago, a party of tinkers quarreled and fought, first among themselves, and then with some Tiree villagers. In the excitement, a tinker's wife threw off her cap and allowed her hair to fall over her shoulders in wild disorder. She then bared her knees, and falling to the ground in a praying attitude, poured forth a torrent of curses that struck awe into all who heard her. She invoked her evil imprecation, 'Drowning by sea and con- flagration on land! May you never see a son to follow your body to the graveyard, or a daughter to mourn your death! I have made my wish before this, and I will make it now, and there was not yet a day I did not see my wish fulfilled!"

In medieval times a witch's curse was on persons, their herds, flocks and crops. In the Scottish Highlands a person under a curse or spell was believed to be powerless over his own will, to be living but moving and acting as if in a trance. Death was the ultimate of all curses.

POWER OF SPELLS

The power of the spoken word is unquestionable by most primitive people, especially if used by a person well known to be versed in the art of magic. When the words are couched in an unknown language it further adds to the belief. The magicians of Ancient Egypt employed gibberish to impress and confuse those listening to their incantations. The practice was also used by the magicians and sorcerers of the Middle Ages as well as by the medicine men of the North American Indians.

Over the centuries spells were created into established formulas. As they proved effective they remained and were recorded. In Ancient Egypt not only were the spells well formulated, but the tone of voice to be used was also prescribed. It is conceded by those knowledgeable in the art of the occult that the power of a spell remains in force until such time as the energy of the spell is neutralized.

An important prerequisite to formulating a spell is the maker's belief in its effectiveness. Today in our more primitive societies, hexing, cursing and projecting spells are still being practiced. From what we know of Voodooism, practiced primarily in the Caribbean, a forceful curse creates a great deal of trouble for the recipient. Again, as in Ancient Egypt, the curse or spell is phrased in an established format, and is delivered with strong emotion and exaggerated body motion. The more absolute belief the witch doctor has in his spell, the greater will be its effectiveness.

Even in our Western culture the curse is acknowledged. In the opera, *Rigoletto*, the court jester, Rigoletto, incurs the wrath of the Count of Monterone who angrily curses the intemperate jester. From that moment on, Rigoletto is a changed man and fears the worst. At the end of the tragic opera, Rigoletto falls to his knees and exclaims, 'The curse is fulfilled!'

HEXING IN OUR TIME

Similar to a spell, a hex is a powerful negative thought form. A thought expressed with a strong emotional outburst is the key to the effectiveness of a hex. The more energy used in the ritual of hexing, the more effective is the hex. The emotions are generated in the subconscious where all the work is done. Once the subconscious has been unequivocally convinced something will happen, it happens. To enter into a highly emotional state to implement a hex, the witch-doctor who practices hexing may use drums, exaggerated physical rituals and drugs.

Hexing is characterized by loss of appetite and consequent loss of weight. Frequently, such persons do not wish to drink. As the body continues to deteriorate, it can lead to death.

All hexing performed by a witch-doctor is not usually considered evil. In certain primitive societies it is the duty of the witch-doctor to punish a malefactor who has committed a crime not punished by law. However, if a practitioner of hexing wishes evil to come to another and then proceeds on his own initiative to put on a hex upon that person, it may well back-fire on him. Performing an act without moral justification draws a corresponding negative response back to the creator of that act. An incautious witch-doctor may well experience dire consequences of the hex meant for another.

Max Freedom Long, researcher of the Hawaiian Huna religion, tells of an incident involving a Kahuna priest whose hex backfired on him. The story is referred to as the death wish.

The Kahuna warned a young man of his village not to associate with the white man. The youth did not heed the warning and was hired as a porter with a research expedition headed by Dr. William Tufts Brigham, curator of the Bishop Museum in Honolulu.

Shortly after the expedition began the young man became ill. First, he lost all sensation in his feet and then in his legs. When his lower abdomen began to lose feeling, the Hawaiians present warned Dr. Brigham what was happening and the certain approaching death.

Dr. Brigham, no stranger to Kahuna power, began to reverse the process. He convinced the entities, who were drawing the energy from the victim, that they should desist and turn their attention to the Kahuna. The young man improved and shortly became completely well. Soon afterwards, it was reported that the Kahuna had died.

One does not have to believe in the power of hexing to be hexed. Two prominent psychiatrists worked with the Uruba tribe in West Africa. Dr. Raymond Prince of McGill University and his associate, Dr. Charles Savage, offended a witch doctor. They were hexed. Contrary to their disbelief in hexing, unceasing troubles, ill health and misfortune became their lot. After suffering for months, the hexes were recognized and subsequently neutralized, enabling them to returned to normal. Only then did they fully appreciate the mental power of the witch doctor. They had learned a severe lesson the hard way.

THE DOLL AND THE WITCH

In parts of the Caribbean, Africa and South America, the witch doctor or shaman is regarded as a priest with awesome power. Persons, knowledgeable in the lore of witchcraft, are careful not to anger the priest for fear that a curse from him will bring them harm. The harm may be in the form of economic disaster, ill health or even death. Europeans or North Americans who have no knowledge of such powers frequently come to grief when they inadvertently incur the ire of such a priest. A Nigerian student, working on his doctorate, related to me the following story.

"In our household we had to be very careful whom we hired as a servant. We avoided servants from our village as they could be used by others to harm us with black magic. We would look for a servant from another tribe who more than likely would be unknown to the local people. Such a stranger would be relatively free from pressures by our enemies.

"On one occasion we were unfortunate. Without warning, my brother, a man with a university degree, began acting as a dog. He went about the streets on hands and feet, naked, eating scraps of food or whatever he could find. He slept in the gutters. For a year we desperately searched for the cause. Finally, we found a rag doll well hidden under the floor of our house. This doll was the representation of my brother, cursed by an unknown witch. Possibly my brother had offended the witch. More than likely the witch was paid by an enemy of my brother to put on the spell. Without delay the doll was destroyed and just as suddenly my brother returned to his normal self." (I failed to inquire just how the doll was destroyed.)

Frequently, an effigy resembling a person is made with the intent of directing abuse upon that person through its representation. The effigy is considered one and the same as the person and the malignant thoughts often act much in the same way as a hex. Among some primitive people photographs are forbidden as a person's photograph could be used by an enemy to direct a hex on him. Should a hex be placed on a person via a photograph, the clearing process removes the negative energy from both person and photograph.

Emigrating into this country at this time - legally or illegally - are large numbers of people from the Caribbean Islands. Immigrants from Cuba, Haiti, Dominican Republic, and from the other islands bring with them their Afro-Christian religion. Typically, followers are Roman Catholics with a strong belief in the power of the spirit world. Their spiritual leaders usually are trance mediums who communicate with and seek the help of a variety of spirit entities. Such entities usually identify themselves as a saint or ancient god of an African religion. As these people increase in number and in political and economic power, we may see more evidence in this country of the symptoms of hexes, spells and unexplained psychic phenomena.

HOW TO NEUTRALIZE A HEX

An extreme negative thought-form could be called a spell or hex. It is most effective when delivered with a vehement outburst of energy. This furnishes the key to neutralizing the effect of such energy.

A hex can be neutralized by utilizing the same technique used to create the hex. A strong positive mental visualization, delivered with emotion, erases the effect of a hex.

In most instances, negative hexing is done inadvertently. A strong negative emotional thought acts in the same way as a hex. Conversely, it is removed by a strong positive emotional thought.

HOW TO CHANGE A PERSON

When an exorcism of spirit possession has been done and little if any changes in the subject are observed, we can suspect other causes. In particular, there may be persons involved who are projecting their negative thoughts toward the subject. Most often the person projecting such thoughts or energy toward another is not aware he is doing it. He does not know, for instance, that he is the cause of the antisocial behavior of the subject. Neither is the subject usually aware of the source of his problem. The following story well illustrates the damaging effects of negative energies and how they were neutralized.

EXPECTANCY

An interesting case of negative thinking occurred between a mother and her daughter, age 14. Often, the mother had complained to me about her highly emotional daughter.

Typically the mother said, "When my daughter enters the house, she immediately explodes her anger, deprecation and abuse upon me. Nothing will satisfy her. In her eyes, everything I do, is wrong! I simply don't know what to do with her!"

Finally, after listening to the complaints for some time, I removed the opaque glasses from my consciousness. I concluded the mother expected her daughter to be nasty to her and was unconsciously projecting that negative thought to the girl. The thought in the form of negative energy was exploding back to the mother!

The solution was simple. The mother needed to change her attitude and thinking about her daughter. I explained to the mother what was happening and suggested that she think of her daughter as being a loving, considerate and an all-right person. The mother agreed to try the experiment. A month later the mother expressed surprise how much her daughter had changed. 'I can hardly believe she is the same person!' she exclaimed.

DETECTING NEGATIVE ENERGIES

As important as an exorcism is, to identify and neutralize hexes and negative thought forms may be even more important. An extreme negative thought-form, for all practical purposes, is a curse or hex. The negative thoughts, for instance, which Lena's son was unconsciously projecting toward his father, is a common example of negative energy that causes so much distress. (See Chapter 5) Refer to *Thought Forms* by Annie Besant and C.W. Leadbeater for more on this subject.

Negative energies are difficult to detect. Identification of their source is even more difficult. Such energies often affect the subject in very much the same way as a negative possessing spirit. When a person is cleared of possessing entities and still displays antisocial behavior, negative energies are suspect. When the source of the energy is known, the effect can be readily eradicated. Dr. Edward Jastram makes these comments in *Body, Mind and Spirit* (p.239)

"Given the possibility of these negative influences, the next problem is to detect them and then clear them. Detection of the presence of negative energies can be accomplished in different ways, depending upon individual skills. Some people are able to see or visualize them; some can sense their presence. Some can detect and 'measure' them by dowsing with a pendulum.

There may be other methods. In any event, it is desirable when dealing with this problem to be able to define what the negative influences are, how many are present, and the relative intensity of their influence on the conscious and subconscious aspects of personality."

CLEARING NEGATIVE ENERGIES

The more we can convince our subconscious that an event is taking place in the now time, the more likely it will occur. The more vivid the picturization, greater will be the impression on the subconscious. A physical demonstration further convinces the subconscious of the reality of the event. Gestures and symbolic visualizations can be used to create the objectives desired. Hexing, as practiced in Voodooism, uses similar procedures.

To neutralize negative put-on energies, I utilize a procedure identical to hexing. I use a vivid and forceful demonstration to impress unequivocally my subconscious mind. Using my hands, arms and body for emphasis, I project the following picturization:

'Around this person I visualize a black cloud which is the attracted negative energy. This cloud is now rising. It is turning into a dark purple, now it is violet. The cloud is dispersing back to the sender but now in the form of love. A soft white light now glows around this person, giving complete protection from all negative energies.'

By using strong positive imaging, negative energies can be neutralized in countless other ways. Don't limit your imagination.

Similar to negative energies are negative programs which act upon a person. Using the pendulum to get answers to questions and the convenient Parametric Chart, you can ask how many negative programs a person has accumulated. These may be deprivations programs of childhood, anger programs or fear programs. In John Van Drie's analysis, (Chapter 9) he does not distinguish between spirit entities, negative energies or negative programs. He exorcised them all at the same time with quite satisfactory results. To neutralize negative programs I use the following effective picturization.

'Upon the head of this person, I see dark spots each representing a negative program. A cleansing torrential rain pours down upon this person. The spots are washed off. The person is now clear of all negative programs.'

PROTECTION

Since spirit personalities are easily attracted, protection must be provided to prevent a recurrence of possession once a person is cleared. If a person slips back into old habits he can attract an entirely new set of earth-bound spirits. Every person has self-will and can select salvation or destruction. That does not mean he should not be given help if available. When the circumstances are known, help can be given.

To avoid a lengthy explanation, the metaphysical **Law of Thought** can effectively be used to check the destructive actions of a person. The law states: **Whatever we think and believe that is what we will experience.** This law can be used for the benefit of others as well as for oneself.

By picturizing and believing good will come into the life of another person, we can create a positive life reality for that person. Also, through the art of metaphysical thinking, a person using visualization can create protective barriers of all sorts to resist invasion of undesirable spirits. Negative energies picked up from others can also be eliminated. Negative programs can be canceled and positive emotions such as harmony, love, happiness and joy can be substituted. Better health, greater personal fulfillment and increased prosperity can result. All of this is ultimately possible. A knowledge of how the mind works is essential in understanding how visualization is used to fulfill one's desires.

As part of the clearing, I build a strong mental picture of protection for the subject. After the possessing spirits have been sent on their way, I place the following positive thought-form around the person cleared:

"Around you I visualize a protective sphere, strong, impenetrable, with ten foot thick walls. Love can pass both ways through these walls. On the outside of this sphere is a highly polished mirror surface which reflects back to its source in the form of love all negative energy of every kind: mental, psychic, or physical."

For those persons who had been keeping company for a long time with strong, negative spirit personalities, I may add the following thought-form:

"Around you is a hot ball of fire, flaming white. This fire will destroy all negative entities directed toward you."

Do not limit your imagination. If you desire, make the subject invisible to spirits. Whatever you believe will work. I then create a thought-form which comes close to resembling a prayer. Picturizing, and feeling the thoughts, I speak:

"At the center of your being I see a brilliant pinpoint of the light of love. It is expanding, covering your entire body with love. It radiates outward, touching all those around you with love, and attracting love to you."

The above positive programming is directed to the subconscious of the subject and when made with concentration and deep feeling it is most effective.

FURTHER THOUGHTS

Very little is known about the psychic forces acting upon us. Nevertheless, there is every indication that our prime protection is the positive mental energy we exert to neutralize whatever negative force exists. The Yogi advocates a white light of protection created by visualization. Others leave the protection up to their guardian angels; many to God. For myself, I am protected in whatever I do and wherever I go by the absolute belief that I am perfectly safe. Sometimes, to further strengthen my belief, I visualize a golden circle of protection around my home and car. I know that they are safe.

We are dealing with a mental process in which energy can be projected to accomplish a destructive purpose. Using our thoughts we can block or neutralize such energies. As with the red brick wall mentally erected by me in London, negative energy can be effectively blocked.

After we have cleared a person of spirit possession, we have done but half the job. It is imperative that all other negative influences around our subject be neutralized. These include hateful and damaging thoughts of others, both of the living and of the dead. It also includes negative thoughts forms as well as the destructive power of hexes and spells. With persistence, study, and patience all can be neutralized.

Once you have evidence that your thoughts can create any condition that you desire, this knowledge can be expanded to achieve far reaching results. The next chapter may stimulate your thinking to go beyond the boundary of traditional beliefs.

CHAPTER 12
Creative Thought

Let us define the hidden meaning of the expression, "Power of positive thinking." Most people think of it as a healthy and satisfactory way of thinking. Nothing magic is attached to it. We like people who think this way. They are far better company than the negative thinkers. Yet, it is more than all these.

Thought is the most powerful creative force in the universe. Our thinking shapes our lives. All that comes to us, good or bad, is caused by our thinking.

The Law: How we think and believe, either in a positive or, negative way, will determine our experience.

The law may be negatively paraphrased: Think bad thoughts and don't be surprised if you fall through an open manhole!

YOUR POWER

With our thinking, we are tapping a Universal Force capable of anything and everything that we can imagine. Imaging is the pathway to reality. In my daily experiences, hardly a day goes by without witnessing a miracle. They really are not miracles as I understand what is happening. Nevertheless, to others, they appear to be miracles. Events are brought into reality by concentrating on the results that I wish to see occur. All action described in this book has been produced by pure thought. Little physical energy was used.

In this work, your desire to help is translated into action by your thinking and visualization. For instance, see negative spirits leaving your client; see him protected from future invasion. Know that he is enjoying a better life with improved health. Picture him feeling joyful and in harmony with all about him. It will take but a few minutes of your time. The change for the better often will be without precedent.

Advanced spiritual entities on the other side have access to the great political leaders of this world. They are at the councils of war; they are with the planners of peace. They are intimates of inventors, and have knowledge of the breakthroughs achieved in the research laboratories throughout the world. When we ask for guidance, whether it be from these enlightened souls or come from a Universal Source, we should accept the truth as tapping an infinite library of knowledge. We may simply accept the premise that there are exalted beings on the other side, ready and willing to help us.

Whether we are aware of it or not, much of the guidance we receive is from the spirit world. When we quiet our mind during a meditation period or in a moment of relaxation, often original and useful ideas will come to us. Thoughts will come even though often we will not be able to identify their source. Such thoughts are often fleeting and when they come, it is wise to promptly make a note of them.

POWER OF LOVE

Love, in the affairs of mankind, is like grease to the wheels of a locomotive; without it nothing moves forward. When building your aspirations and directions on love, your life has a total new meaning, resulting in enormous changes for good. Your love becomes the causal driving force to bring about positive events that have no dimensions or limitations.

Universal Force can be used either to produce a negative or positive result. Unconditional love cannot be used other than to produce a positive result. Love is a powerful tool which when used conquers all that is evil or ignorant. One who freely gives love without preconditions, cannot be said to suffer from an extended ego.

In an exorcism it is just as important, perhaps more, to be concerned for the welfare of the invisible spirit entities as you would be for your client. These spirit people come from every walk of life, have a broad spectrum of beliefs and are of every race and age. Some lived as far back as thousands of years, others in our own time. Their individualized experience when living, were the traditional poor man, rich man, scholar, soldier and thief. They have one thing in common. They are stuck here in this plane and desperately wish to know what to do, what to believe and where to go. More than likely when living, nobody gave them direction or an indication what they would find after dying. A possession may be their sole option. You, by your love and compassion, provide the key to the release of these unguided souls.

Your concern for the lost ones, who may number in the hundreds at a single exorcism, become the hammer and chisel in breaking the chains of their bondage on earth. You have just as truly freed these people as you would have freed prisoners from the darkest, most fearful dungeon on earth. You have also done something even greater. You have given the least spiritually developed entities among them perhaps their first glimpse what unselfish love can do. You have made the first inroad in their consciousness that love, with all its powers, does exist.

The immortal philosopher and psychologist, William James, (1840-1910) succinctly expressed the satisfaction one finds in doing this work: "At times you will have results so thrilling, so alluring that no amount of patient drudgery will seem to have been too high a price to pay. As the work proceeds, the evident harvest will be increasingly demonstrated."

RESCUE WORK

Some years ago, I was intrigued with Rescue Work. This is directing a lost spirit to his next level of development where he can be given guidance and instruction. It is where he can be among friends and family in the spirit world.

After I had first understood there was a spirit world, I wanted to know more about it. After much reading, I learned that there were disembodied spirits of the dead, called earthbound spirits, who are hopelessly lost. I understood some had been wandering on the earth plane for hundreds of years, some perhaps thousands. I had asked myself, 'How could I help them?' I was given the answer when I learned the technique of performing an exorcism.

An exorcism accomplishes two important functions. First, the troubled earthly victim is cleared allowing him to function with free will. Secondly, the nearby spirit persons are sent to a place where they have the opportunity to evolve spiritually. This is rescue work. Be gentle and considerate with them. They are in an unfortunate situation in need of guidance and instruction. The spirit entity helped may well be a close beloved relative or dear friend. Whether you can identify the spirit or not, you are rendering a vital service to those who dwell in the lower astral plane, those who are earthbound.

HARMONY

A sense of harmony and peace of mind is more important to an individual than any single material thing or circumstance. When a person has achieved this state, all events that create disharmony have no power over the individual. Personal relationships, condition of one's finances, state of health, one's job, home and business environment, all coexist in harmony with one another.

Picturization of harmony in a person's life strengthens personal relationships. It can establish better understanding between adversaries. A complete turnabout of an unfavorable situation can often occur within hours.

A treatment for harmony could be the single most important service that you could render another. In reference to the case entitled, The Safe Divorce, page 18, the depossession was but partly responsible for the successful outcome.

Before concluding the clearing process, I give a treatment for harmony to those involved. I express the following with feeling and picturization:

"I visualize you standing in a circle of your family and friends. There is joy in your hearts, a smile on your lips. There is complete understanding, each for the other. There is compassion and trust for one another. There is an all embracing love; there is complete harmony. There is peace of mind knowing all is well with this wonderful group of people. All are truly grateful and thankful for this wonderful feeling."

The above visualization can be as powerful as an exorcism. When an exorcism does not produce the expected results, in most instances a treatment for harmony will achieve a final breakthrough.

In world affairs as well as in personal affairs, harmony is the key for world peace. Peace Pilgrim who dedicated her life to peace, peace within, peace among people and peace among nations, offers this sound advice: "This is the way of peace: Overcome evil with good, falsehood with truth and hatred with love. The Golden Rule would do as well. Please don't say lightly that these are just religious concepts and are not practical. These are laws governing human conduct, which apply as rigidly as the laws of gravity. When we disregard these laws in any walk of life, chaos results. Through obedience to these laws this frightened, war weary world of ours could enter into a period of peace and richness of life beyond our fondest dreams."

SPIRITUAL HEALING

For ten years I have been a minister of spiritual healing. I have spent hundreds of hours giving healing. I receive little or no remuneration for the work, for the successes achieved have been compensation enough. A healer taps the source of Healing Power and directs the healing to the person needing healing. Not to pass up any opportunity to give healing where needed, I devised a simple method to project healing to one or to, a hundred persons at once.

In the pendulum analysis I determine the state of health of each person, expressed as a percentage. For those needing healing, I close my eyes and speak softly to myself:

"I see all the people standing in front of me. There is a strong white light of healing covering their entire bodies. This healing light penetrates to each cell in their bodies, healing all cells from head to toe." To fix my concentration I equate the white light to the power of healing.

The secret of spiritual healing is to enter the alpha level or subconscious concentrating on the intention to heal. Once that level is achieved, contact is made with the Superconscious and the healing is done. Contact can be anywhere between ten seconds to one minute. This is a simple procedure, but the results are often phenomenal.

A description of a healing would better describe the procedure. Two cases come to mind. The first involved a man in Poland who had a stroke and became paralyzed on the right side of his body. When his estranged wife in this country heard the sad news she immediately sent money to Poland to secure the best medical aid for her husband. A few days passed and the news was not good. Hospitalize, he had lost the capacity to talk and walk and was unable to leave his bed. As the wife appeared to be most distressed, I asked her if she would like me to project healing to her husband. Although she knew little about spiritual healing she gratefully consented.

I sat down in the nearest chair, certainly not a comfortable one, and closed my eyes and relaxed. Taking a few slow deep breaths, to aid relaxation I then concentrated my attention on a man in a hospital bed in Poland, a man whom I had never met, nor had ever seen. I had no idea what he looked like. To aid my concentration I visualized a white light of healing covering the man's body. I'm sure a light of any color would have done just as well. In less than a minute my mind slipped into the alpha range of vibration and a few seconds afterwards I was asleep. Awaking in about 20 minutes I had the distinct impression that the patient had improved. I voiced my opinion that he would soon be able to move his toes. We were not prepared for what happened. The next day he walked out of the hospital!

Another request for healing was even more dramatic. Rachel 0. had worked 30 years for our company and held a responsible position as Quality Control Supervisor. At a hospital her husband was dreadfully ill with cancer. Rachel spent three weeks at the bedside of her dying and pain ridden husband. Finally, exhausted, she could no longer endure the torture of seeing him in constant pain. She called her friend, Lenore 0. at our factory to ask me to intercede on his behalf. Lenore explained to me that Rachel was at the end of her strength and had asked healing for the dying man. "Sure," I replied, "let's do it right now." Seated at my desk, I closed my eyes and took a few deep breaths to relax. I then concentrated on a white light of healing covering the patient in the hospital. I had not been told where the hospital was. After a minute or so I slipped into the alpha state of total concentration. Immediately I had a strong feeling that the man was no longer in pain and when opening my eyes told this to Lenore.

As Lenore walked out of my office I called to her and

requested, "Please note the time." It was 3:05 PM. Later we heard that the husband had died precisely at 3:00 PM, exactly at the time of the healing!

Rachel's husband was beyond any medical help. The medicine administered to relieve the pain was ineffective. The man was dying. The healing cut short his pain and his inevitable death was no longer prolonged.

The subject of healing, whether it be called psychic healing, spiritual healing or called by a dozen other names, is an involved topic and a hundred or more books have been written on it. I assure the reader that healing does occur so often as to exclude coincidence. I refer you to the late Harry Edwards, recognized as England's greatest spiritual healer of this century. At the Harry Edwards Spiritual Healing Sanctuary there are records of thousands of persons who have received successful healing from him during his lifetime. His methods of healing are simple and practiced by countless healers in this country as well as abroad. His work is being continued by Joan and Ray Branch and their trained staff in Shere, Surrey, England. For more on this subject, refer to *Guide to the Understanding and Practice of Spiritual Healing* by Harry Edwards. (See the bibliography)

It may be appropriate to perform additional picturizations to cover special needs. Should a person have an alcohol or drug problem, I visualize him detesting and rejecting all alcohol or addictive drugs. I see him having nothing to do with others who drink excessively or who are addicts. If a person is broke and out of work, I visualize that person feeling prosperous and working at a job which gives him much satisfaction. This process is described in considerable detail in my book, *The Power of Thought*. (See the bibliography.)

A LOOK INTO THE FUTURE

I have witnessed the gradual acceptance by the medical profession that hypnotism is a reality and not an illusion. In the 1920's hypnotism was practiced for entertainment, not for therapeutic use. Today hypnotism is being used as a valuable tool in the diagnosis of mental problems. Every knowledgeable psychologist uses it. Today, similar to hypnotism, the medical profession is gradually becoming aware that spirit possession also has validity. Some psychologists who understand its reality are achieving astonishing results in altering troublesome personalities.

There is every indication that within the next five or ten years the examination and analysis by psychologists of persons who are suspected of being spirit possessed will become routine. Methods such as described in this book will be used to clear those who are possessed. To achieve a level of acceptance, the nomenclature may have to be changed. Hypnotism had been called Mesmerism and before that, animal magnetism. Today, to the medical profession, the term 'multiple personality' is more acceptable than the term 'spirit possession'. Names are not important; methods to achieve satisfactory results are. We are beginning to open our eyes and to cast aside our prejudices. Slowly, but with deliberation, we shall find simple solutions to complex problems.

I wish to remind you, the reader, that everything described in this book can be done by you. You need but the desire and the dedication to do it.

FRONTIERS

Working with the laws of the spirit world (Chapter 4) and with your knowledge of exorcism, the scope for potential accomplishment is almost limitless. Think of the possibilities of clearing the criminals you read about in the newspapers. How about taking on a whole prison? You may wish to concentrate your attention on a section of your city that enjoys less than a good reputation. Such an idea is not fantastic. It is within your ability to do so.

A mind control group targeted the whole state of Rhode Island to reduce the number of automobile accidents. The group used only the power of the mind and visualization. It resulted in a 45 percent decline in accidents for a six-month test period. As expected, the state authorities discounted the results.

If you are involved in a social group, check the members who appear to be inconsistent in their actions or thoughts. They may be possessed or influenced by the negative thinking of persons unknown to you. You can be of considerable service by clearing them. You can also observe at first hand the results of your work.

When you are ready for greater challenges you can consider political groups. Start with your local governing body. Clearing those who have a problem can improve your city government. With that done, you may wish to examine your state governor and his staff. You can check the state legislature and the judicial body for possession. The federal government can also be your target. You will be surprised to learn of the relatively high percentage of persons in public office who are possessed.

Our mental institutions are full of persons who are possessed. More than half of them exhibit some symptom of multiple personality, MPD. If one person, diagnosed as a schizophrenic, can be brought back into the real world, how many more are there who also can be helped? (See Chapter 7, *Healing Blocks*). As a practicing exorcist, you may some day have the opportunity of emptying the mental ward of your local hospital.

You may be ready to tackle problems on an international level. You already have an idea how to neutralize terrorists and hijackers. What would happen if you exorcised the heads of state of nations at war? Consider the possibilities of exorcising warring armies, officers and soldiers. Don't limit yourself.

Now and then you will get a glimpse of the results accomplished by the work you are doing. An unexpected reversal of deleterious action will give you a strong indication that you have done something. As nothing is really coincidental, your initiative can effect the life of one person or a thousand. Some day you, too, may author a book describing the miraculous results of your efforts and discoveries.

The author is available to answer questions or to give assistance. You may forward your inquiries to the publisher.

Bibliography

Albright, Peter, M.D., *Body Mind and Spirit*, 1980, The Stephen Greene Press, Brattleboro, VT 05301

Bach, Marcus, *Strange Altars*, 1952, Bobbs-Merrill Co., Inc. Publishers, Indianapolis, IN

Bagnall, Oscar, *The Origin and Properties of the Human Aura*, 1970, University Books, Inc., New York, NY

Bander, Peter, *Voices from the Tapes*, 1973, Drake Publishers, Inc, 381 Park Ave, New York NY 10016

Behrend, Genevieve, *Your Invisible Power*, DeVorss & Company Publishers, P.O. Box 550, Marina Del Rey, CA 90251

Bendit, Laurence J, *The Mirror of Life and Death*, 1965, Theosophical Publishing House, P.O. Box 270, Wheaton, Il 60187

Besant, A, and C.W. Leadbeater, *Thought Forms*, 1925, Theosophical Publishing House, P.O. Box 270, Wheaton, IL 60187

Bird, Christopher, *The Divining Hand*, 1979, E.P. Dutton Publishers, 2 Park Ave., New York, NY 10016

Burke, Jane Revere, *Let Us In*, 1931, E.P. Dutton Publishers, 2 Park Ave., New York, NY 10016

Butler, W.E., *How to Develop Clairvoyance*, 1970, The Aquarian Press, 37/38 Margaret St., London, W. 1

Cox, Bill, *Techniques of Pendulum Dowsing*, 1977, Bill & Davina Cox, P.O. Box 30561, Santa Barbara, CA 93130

Crookall, Robert, *The Next World and the Next*, 1966, Theosophical Publishing House, P.O. Box 270, Wheaton, IL 60187

Edwards, Harry, *A Guide to the Understanding and Practice of Spiritual Healing*, 1974, The Healer Publishing Company, Ltd., Burrows Lea, Shere, Guildford, Surry, England

Evans-Wentz, W.Y., *The Tibetan Book of the Dead*, 1960, Oxford University Press, London, England

Farthing, Geoffrey, *When We Die*, 1968, The Theosophical Publishing House, P.O. Box 270, Wheaton, Il 60187

Finch, Elizabeth & William, *The Pendulum and Your Health*, 1977, P.O. Box 177, Fairacres, NM 88033

Finch, William, *Pendulum and Possession*, 1975, Treasure Chest, 1050 W. Grant Rd., Suite 101, Tucson, AZ 85703

Fiore, Edith, Ph.D., *The Unquiet Dead*, 1987, Doubleday & Company, Inc., Garden City, NY

Fiore, Edith, Ph.D., *You Have Been Here Before*, Coward, McCann & Geoghegan, Inc. New York, NY

Ford, Arthur, *The Life Beyond Death* 1971, G.P. Putnam's Sons, 200 Madison Ave., New York, NY 10016

Hampton, Charles, *The Transition Called Death*, 1943, Publishing House, P.O. Box 270, Wheaton, IL 60187

Hayes, Patricia & Marshall Smith, *Extension of Life*, 1986, Dimensional Brotherhood Publishing House, P.O. Box 768153, Roswell, GA 30076

Hill, Dawn, *Reaching for the Other Side*, 1983, Newcastle Publishing Company, Inc., North Hollywood, CA

Holliwell, Raymond, Ph.D., *Working with the Law*, 1964, School of Christian Philosophy, 3121 N. 60th St., Phoenix, AZ

Holmes, Ernest. Ph.D., *Science of Mind*, 1938, 44th Printing, Dodd, Mead and Co., 79 Madison Ave., New York, NY 10016

Holmes, Jesse Herman, M.D., *As We See It From Here*, 1980, Metascience Corp, Publication Division., P.O. Box 747, Franklin, NC 28734

Jacobson, Nils O., M.D., *Life Without Death?* 1971, Dell Publishing Company, 1 Dag Hammarskjold Plaza, New York, NY 10017

Kilner, Walter J., *The Human Aura*, 1965, University Books, Inc., New Hyde Park, NY 11040

Kilner, Walter J., *Thought Forms*, University Books, Inc., New Hyde Park, NY 11040

Krippner, Stanley, & Daniel Rubin, *The Kirlian Aura*, 1974, Doubleday & Company, Inc., Garden City, NY

Kubler-Ross, Elizabeth, M.D., *Death, the Final Stage of Growth*, 1975, Prentice-Hall, Inc., Englewood Cliffs, NJ 07632

Leadbeater, C.W., *The Astral Plane*, 1973, Theosophical Publishing House, P.O. Box 270, Wheaton, IL 60187

Leadbeater, C.W., *Clairvoyance*, 1899, Theosophical Publishing House, P.O. Box 270, Wheaton, Il 60187

Leadbeater, C.W., *The Life After Death*, 1979, Theosophical Publishing House, P.O. Box 270, Wheaton, Il 60187

Leadbeater, C.W., *The Other Side of Death*, 1904, Theosophical Publishing House, P.O. Box 270, Wheaton, Il 60187

Leftwich, Robert H., *Dowsing*, 1977, The Aquarian Press, Wellingborough, Northamptonshire, England

Lhermitte, Jean, M.D., *True and False Possession*, 1963, Hawthorn Books, Publishers, New York, NY.

Long, Max Freedom, *The Secret Science Behind Miracles*, 1948, DeVorss & Co., 1641 Lincoln Blvd., Santa Monica, CA 90404

Maurey, Eugene, *Power of Thought*, 1984, Midwest Press, 4557 W. 60th St., Chicago, IL 60629

Meek, George, *After We Die, What Then?*, 1980, Metascience Corp. Publishing Division, P.O. Box 747, Franklin, NC 28734

Mermet, Abbe, *Principles & Practice of Radiesthesia*, 1975, Watkins Publishing, 45 Lower Belgrave St., London SW1W OLT, England

Moody, Raymond A., M.D., *Life After Life*, 1975, Bantam Books, Inc. 666 Fifth Ave., New York, NY 10019

Montgomery, Ruth, *Here and Hereafter*, 1968, Fawcett Publications, Inc, Greenwich, CN

Payne, Phoebe D. & Laurence J. Bendit, *This World and That*, 1950. Theosophical Publishing House, P.O. Box 270 Wheaton, Il 60187

Peace Pilgrim, *An Autobiography*, 1983, Compiled by her friends. Ocean Tree Press, P.O. Box 1295, Santa Fe, NM 87501

Peck, M. Scott, M.D., *People of the Lie*, 1983, Simon & Schuster, 1230 Avenue of the Americas, New York, NY 10020

Pike, James A., *The Other Side*, 1968, Doubleday & Company, Inc., Garden City, NY

Powell, Arthur E., *The Astral Body*, 1972, Theosophical Publishing House, P.O. Box 270, Wheaton, IL 60187

Randall, Neville, *Life After Death*, Hunt Barnard Printing Ltd., Transworld Publishers Ltd., 61-63 Uxbridge Road, Ealing, London WS 5SA England.

Regush, Nicholas, *The Human Aura,* 1977, Berkley Publishing Corp. 200 Madison Avenue, New York, NY 10016

Rhine, J.B., Ph.D., *New Frontiers of the Mind,* 1942, World Publishing Co., Cleveland, OH 44114

Rogo, D. Scott, *The Infinite Boundary,* 1987, Dodd, Mead & Co., 71 Fifth Ave., New York, NY 10003

Sabom, Michael, M.D., *Recollections of Death,* Harper and Row Publishers, Inc. New York, NY 10022

Sherman, Harold, H., *The Dead Are Alive,* 1981, Amherst Press, Amherst, WI 54406

Sherman, Harold, H., *You Can Communicate with the Unseen World,* 1974, Fawcett Publications, Inc., Greenwich, CT 06830

Sherman, Harold, H., *You Live After Death,* 1972, Fawcett Publications, Inc., P.O. Box 1014, Greenwich, CT 06830

Sherman, Harold H. & Sir Hubert Wilkins. *Thoughts Through Space,* 1942, Amherst Press, Amherst, WI 54406

Siedersberger, Ludwig, *Experience of a Dowser,* 1982, Canadian Society of Geobiology and Biomagnetism, 5854 Swayze Drive, Niagara Falls, Ontario, Canada L2G 3V9

Spraggett, Allen & William V. Rauscher, *Arthur Ford: The Man Who Talked with the Dead,* 1973, The New American Library, Inc., 1301 Avenue of the Americas, New York, NY 10019

Sullivan, Eileen, *Arthur Ford Speaks from Beyond,* J. Philip O'Hara, Inc., 20 East Huron, Chicago, IL 60611

Welch, William A., *Talks with the Dead,* 1975, Pinnacle Books, New York, NY

Wickland, Carl A., M.D., *Thirty Years Among the Dead,* 1974, Newcastle Publishing, 1521 N. Vine St., Hollywood, CA 90028

Wilson, C.W.M., M.D., Ph.D., *Entity Possession: A Causative Factor in Disease,* 1987, Psionnic Medicine, VI (23) 4-21, Scotland.

Wilson, C.W.M., M.D., Ph.D., *The Association Between Allergic Disease, Entities, Multiple Personalities and Medical Dowsing,* 1987, Alternative Medicine, Scotland

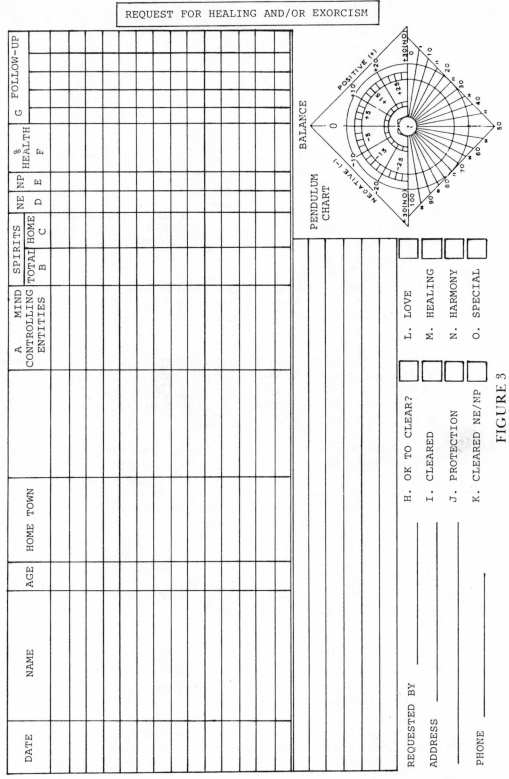

REQUEST FOR HEALING AND/OR EXORCISM

FIGURE 3

Print all data.
Give approximate age and town.
Include your address if you wish a report.

REV. GENE MAUREY
4555 W. 60th ST.
CHICAGO, IL 60629

EXPLANATIONS OF ITEMS ON FIGURE 3

A. These personalities are spirit entities who have entered the mind of the individual and to a large extent are controlling the thoughts and actions of that person.

B. The total spirit entities include column A and other personalities attracted to the person who follow that person wherever he goes. They usually do not have the person's best interest in mind.

C. In old single dwelling residences and in older apartment buildings, there are spirit personalities who inhabit such buildings. They like such places and usually cause no trouble. They know of no other place to go.

D. Negative energies are those forces impinging upon a person, causing that person to be mentally disturbed with accompanying misfortune. These energies are projected by a person toward another with negative intentions. They are similar to hexes put on by voodoo witch doctors.

E. Negative programming are subconscious habits of thought we have learned through faulty interpretation of our experiences, usually when we were a child. They may have been caused by deprivation such as by lack of food, security or love. They may have been caused by fear, fear of the dark, fear of imagined monsters, or fear of violence of any sort. Also, negative programming can be caused by anger toward a sister or brother, jealousy or envy toward others, or indoctrined anger placed there by a parent against a race, religion or nationality.

F. 100% health occurs usually at birth or shortly thereafter. For a person of 40 years of age, the following percentage health rating is used:

100% to 90% Excellent   65% to 55% Good   35% to 25% Poor
85% to 75% Very Good   50% to 40% Fair   20% & Below Critical

It is assumed that a person under 18 with a rating of 55% would not be in good health.

G. A person has free will and may continue his bad habits after he has been cleared. *Follow-up is necessary to insure a more stable personality.*

The check list at the bottom of the page are those special treatments which are beneficial to the client. See page entitled "Treatments".

The pendulum chart is used to dowse specific data about an individual. The lower half is used for percentages and to determine quantities. The upper left hand quadrant is used to identify the characteristics of mind controlling entities. The upper right hand quadrant is used to identify the personality of positive entities. See page entitled "Evaluation of Spirit Entities".

DESCRIPTIONS OF TREATMENTS ON FIGURE 3

The following is a brief summary of the treatments given to each person. Although each treatment is done at a distance from the person, years of experience have shown these procedures to be highly effective.

H. OK TO CLEAR?
Using the pendulum I ask of a person's higher self if he/she should be cleared. Almost always the answer is yes.

I. CLEARED
Through a spirit intermediary I contact the possessing spirit entities, explain the situation to them and then send them to their next level of development. Should they be reluctant to leave they are given little opputunity to refuse.

J. PROTECTION
I place a mental sphere of protection around the person, inpenetrable to any physical, mental or psychic force.

K. CLEARED NE/NP
To dispel a negative energy (hex), I visualize such force as a dark cloud about the person, then mentally see this cloud rise and change into the energy of love. Using a slightly different method, the energy in negative programs is also neutralized.

L. LOVE
I visually see a pinpoint of love in the center of a person in the form of white light. I see this light expanding, covering the person and touching all people near with love. Love is attracted to the person.

M. HEALING

Healing is accomplished by visualizing cosmic white light of healing covering the person's body. The light then penetrates to every cell of the person's body and gives these cells healing.

N. HARMONY

To create harmony in a person's life, I visualize that person in a circle of his friends, family, relatives and close associates. There is joy and gladness in their hearts, a smile on their lips. Each has a deep understanding of the other and knows she/he is also understood. Each feels love, compassion, trust, respect, and forgiveness for the other. All are thankful and grateful for the wonderful harmonious feeling they have for each other.

O. SPECIAL

Special treatments are often useful to neutralize alcoholism or use of hard drugs. Also conditions may be desired such as companionship, prosperity or a particular positive event in one's life.

FIGURE 4 EVALUATION OF SPIRIT ENTITIES

Position pendulum over center of chart. Ask: "Is this person Possessed?" Relax, if pendulum swings up and down on the chart, the answer is "Yes"; if sideways, the answer is "No". Ask, "Give me an indication of the strongest negative entity?" Relax. Allow the pendulum to swing by itself to a position on the upper left hand quandrant. Continue until all possessing entities are counted.

N   Normal
B   Balanced

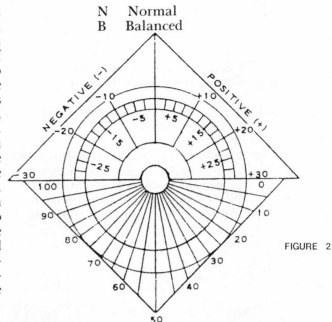

FIGURE 2

A MEASURE OF EVALUATION

Bill Finch in his excellent thesis on spirit possession, *The Pendulum and Possession*, created a yardstick to identify and classify a personality. The personality may be a living person or a spirit entity. The entity may be a possessing spirit. When the exorcist makes a positive identification of the type and strength of the invading spirits, he can be more effective by varying his approach to the exorcism.

On a scale of -30 to +30, using a pendulum, a living person or a spirit entity is analyzed as follows: (Refer to above chart).

  0 Neutral or balanced mind. This is the most sought condition. It is in the majority.

 -5 Has little concern for others or truthfulness. Such a person would make an outstanding used car salesman or politician.

-10 Indicates a basically dishonest tendency, falling between misdemeanor and felony. This person may typically be a shoplifter or petty thief.

-15 Characterized by being involved in car thefts, robberies or similar deeds. May beat his wife and children.

-20 A dangerous criminal. Will commit murder with provocation or when under duress.

-25 Highly dangerous. Will kill with slightest provocation and for little reason.

-30 A mass murderer. Will kill for the love of killing. Needs no reason to kill, nor will anything of a moral nature dissuade the person from killing. (Fortunately for society, and for the exorcist there are not many such spirit entities around. Of some 8000 persons analyzed, I have found but eight with a -30 reading.)

On the other hand, the positive spirit group has some effect on the individual. As a rule they do not cause as much trouble as the negative group. Those rated +20 and greater are troublesome and when removed, the subject is in a better state of mind.

+5 The person has broad thinking and stability; May be a highly qualified teacher or counselor.

+10 A person of great wisdom and sound metaphysical thinking. This person has the attributes of a mystic.

+15 A person firm in ideals and ideas, the typical evangelist.

+20 An intolerant person, inflexible in his/her ideas. Look for a minister determined to reform the congregation.

+25 A person who is stubborn in thought, unrelenting, and unforgiving. The "Hanging Judge."

+30 This is the crusader whose belief is: "Kill it is God's will!"

The above readings are not to be interpreted to mean that a person measuring -15, for instance, will beat his wife or commit a crime. It simply means that under sufficient stress the individual *could* behave in this way.

It is not absolutely necessary to learn everything about a possessing spirit. The above ratings, determined by a pendulum, are usually sufficient.

It will sometimes occur that a strong positive entity will team up with an equally strong negative entity, each not knowing the other is present. The subject is exposed to the worst of both worlds. He may feel no remorse or pangs of conscious. When I make a personality analysis, I check only for negative entities, as even the least negative ones are troublesome. Nevertheless, all other entities present, positive or negative, are counted as a group and cleared as a group.